TO IDENTITY
AND
BEYOND

TO IDENTITY AND BEYOND

PLAY THE LONG GAME
ADVANCE GOD'S KINGDOM
ENJOY ABUNDANT LIFE

MATT PAVLIK MA, LPCC-S
BRINGING YOUR POTENTIAL TO LIGHT

Christian Concepts
New Reflections Counseling, Inc.
Dayton, Ohio, USA

To Identity and Beyond
Copyright © 2018 by Matt Pavlik

All rights reserved. No part of this publication may be reproduced, stored in a retrieval system, or transmitted, in any form or by any means, electronic, mechanical, photocopying, recording, or otherwise, without the written permission of the author.

Published in the United States of America by Christian Concepts (christianconcepts.com), an imprint of New Reflections Counseling, Inc. (newreflectionscounseling.com).

The author offers Internet addresses as suggested resources but does not guarantee the validity of the content. Because of the dynamic nature of the Internet, any links may have changed since publication and may no longer be valid.

Some of the examples are composites from several situations. Details and names have been changed to protect anonymity. Any resemblance to persons alive or dead is purely coincidental.

This book is not intended to be a replacement for professional counseling.

Pavlik, Matthew Edward, 1971-
To Identity and Beyond: Play the Long Game, Advance God's Kingdom, Enjoy Abundant Life / Matt Pavlik.
    ISBN: 978-0-9863831-3-7 (softcover)
    ISBN: 978-0-9863831-4-4 (kindle)
    ISBN: 978-0-9863831-6-8 (epub)
    1. Identity (Psychology) —Religious aspects—Christianity
    2. Shame—Religious aspects—Christianity
    3. Purpose—Religious aspects—Christianity
    4. Self-image—Religious aspects—Christianity

BV4509.5 P38 2018   248.4—dc23

    Self-perception, Truth, Healing, Growth, Self-acceptance, Meaning (Philosophy), Codependency, Addiction, Developmental psychology, Rejection (Psychology), Self-deception

Unless otherwise indicated, all Scripture quotations are from the ESV® Bible (The Holy Bible, English Standard Version®), copyright © 2001 by Crossway, a publishing ministry of Good News Publishers. Used by permission. All rights reserved.

Scripture taken from the Holy Bible, NEW INTERNATIONAL VERSION®, NIV® Copyright © 1973, 1978, 1984, 2011 by Biblica, Inc.® Used by permission. All rights reserved worldwide.

Scripture quotations from THE MESSAGE. Copyright © by Eugene H. Peterson 1993, 1994, 1995, 1996, 2000, 2001, 2002. Used by permission of Tyndale House Publishers, Inc.

Scripture quotations marked (CEV) are from the Contemporary English Version Copyright © 1991, 1992, 1995 by American Bible Society, Used by Permission.

Publishing History

2018 12 08 --- First Edition (print)
2018 12 21 --- First Edition (kindle)
2018 12 21 --- First Edition (epub)

Dedication

To my brothers and sisters in Christ—both present and future.

Ours is the victory in God through Jesus Christ by the Holy Spirit.

The grace of the Lord Jesus Christ, and the love of God, and the fellowship of the Holy Spirit, be with you all.
—2 Corinthians 13:14

CONTENTS

Foreword xi
Preface xiii
Acknowledgments xv

Part I — God's Gift 1
1. Beyond Identity 3
2. What Is Identity? 9
3. What Is Reality? 21
4. From Crisis to Crown 35
5. From Desire to Destiny 45
6. Overcome Opposition 61
7. Establish Trust 79

Part II — Journey to Identity 99
8. Andrew's Journey 101
9. Samantha's Journey 109
10. Olivia's Journey 115

Part III — God's Call 121
11. Identity Maturity 123
12. Stage 1: Caregiver Focused 135
13. Stage 2: Creation Focused 143
14. Stage 3: Crisis Focused 155
15. Stage 4: Christ Focused 167
16. Stage 5: Calling Focused 181
17. Going Beyond 191

Supplemental Material 195
Appendix A — You 2.0 Prayer 197
Appendix B — Identity Affirmations 199
Appendix C — Identity Scriptures 201
Appendix D — Movie List 203
Selected Bibliography 205
Index of Scriptures 207

Foreword

My seminary training prepared me to preach, teach, and lead as a pastor, but there are no shortcuts to getting to know people and their struggles. One of the biggest challenges I encounter as a pastoral caregiver within the local church is helping people to discover their true identities in Jesus Christ. I have served within small, medium, and megachurches, and many of the people I have encountered throughout the years have struggled to embrace their identities with their head and heart, and then walk in them. This is why I'm especially grateful to come across the work of Matt Pavlik. As a Licensed Professional Clinical Counselor and devout Christ-Follower, Matt combines his counseling expertise and experience with his Christian faith.

This is more than just a self-help book that you would find at a bookstore or on an episode of Dr. Phil or Oprah. Matt builds each of his chapters from a scriptural basis, digging into the identity crisis every human being must resolve. He shows us that the discovery of our identity unlocks unimagined possibilities in our lives. Identity takes us beyond our ego or self-image to our greater purpose in advancing the Kingdom of God. But until we come to know our identity, we will never know our purpose. The key is to understand that we were made by Almighty God.

I highly recommend *To Identity and Beyond* for anyone who wants to be challenged in growing in their personal development, identity, and God-given purpose. Don't just read through the chapters, but critically think about your own life and answer the questions that Matt poses at the end of each chapter. Take a personal inventory of your journey and reflect on the next level that God is calling you to in relationship with Him and with others. This book is for anyone who has struggled to understand their identity in the context of their past, their career, or their reputation. This is a work that I will be recommending to many of my parishioners and even colleagues because of its uniqueness. Its combination of the importance of scripture, practical examples, and cognitive theory provides a scholarly resource that can be implemented in everyday life. I would encourage you to journey with a small group of friends or people from your church and participate in a meaningful discussion that can help with life transformation.

I'm personally excited about *To Identity and Beyond* because it will serve as a valuable resource to anyone who has ever struggled with who they are.

Sincerely,

Rev. Dr. Rosario Picardo
Dean of The Chapel, United Theological Seminary
Co-Pastor, Mosaic Church
November 2018

Preface

In my practice as a clinical counselor, people come to me in crisis. They think their crisis is being unhappy with how their lives are going. My first objective is to help them know their real struggle.

I like to divide crises into the fish kind and the caterpillar kind. A fish decides to eat a worm; a caterpillar accepts the challenge to become a butterfly. Both have different risks and rewards.

Most people end up with a fish crisis not realizing there is another option. They've already taken the bait, hoping that their circumstances will change for the better. But the bait turns out to be too good to be true; it has a hook—a painful realization that they've overcommitted to something that can't satisfy their hunger.

My goal for this book is to convince you to accept the challenge of the metamorphosis from caterpillar to butterfly. A butterfly crisis requires work and patience, but the result is incomparably better. Jesus came to set you free from the hook. He wants you to see your potential beyond a caterpillar. To live abundantly, you must recognize you have the power to become a butterfly.

I'm assuming you want to follow God, or you're at least open to the idea. But you're stuck, unable to find your place in the world and the church. I want you to see that your problem isn't your circumstances; your problem is not knowing who you truly are.

The Gospel changes everything. When we accept God's salvation, He no longer sees us as unworthy sinners. But I often encounter Christians who hold onto their old self-image.

We must see ourselves through God's eyes. God considers us as sanctified and perfected, even though His work in us is an ongoing process:

We have been sanctified through the offering of the body of Jesus Christ once for all. For by a single offering he has perfected for all time those who are being sanctified.
—Hebrews 10:10, 14

In correcting our self-image, we need to have a clear picture of the God who made us. God is almighty—eternally self-sufficient. The enemy twists this fact to attempt to make us dull, despondent, and defeated. *You don't really matter to God; you're on your own.* While God is able to carry on and enact His will without us, He chooses not to. He desires to take our shame, self-pity, and self-deprecation and make us His sons and daughters.

Until you see yourself as worthwhile, you'll underestimate your significance and limit your contribution to God's kingdom. You must throw off your worthlessness and fully embrace the reality and identity God has for you.

Look to your past to be thankful you're saved. You can be overjoyed because you're a new creation who is free from sin and an eternal death. Look to the future to remain assured of a glorious victory. But don't neglect to look to the present where you can make a significant difference.

God has a specific purpose for your existence. You're a unique creation, so your active participation is essential. He chose to make you a vital part of His plans, part of the body of Christ. In the reality that God has created, each of us is irreplaceable. He desires fellowship with us and wants to see us thrive. It is in this sense that God needs us. If none of us were to rise up to do His bidding, He could make the rocks cry out, but that's not going to happen. God made us to praise Him and praise Him we will.

God has great plans for you, but you can't accomplish anything apart from God. We need God's strength and determination to work in and through us, just as Jesus relied on His Father throughout His life. When we participate by faith, God empowers us. Instead of passively waiting for God to topple the giants in your life, consider that He may be calling you to fight, as David did, with the strength of God's Spirit within you.

Since God has committed to partnering with us to the very end, don't hesitate to step out in faith to discover who you are and to seek to advance God's kingdom. To this end, I invite you to identity and beyond.

Acknowledgments

Thanks to God, who created me and empowers me to complete His work.

Thanks to my parents for their dedication to pray as I follow God's calling.

Thanks to my clients, who teach me every day how to be a better counselor.

Thanks to Will Alejandro, who helped me talk through what I wanted to say.

Thanks to the following test readers who provided feedback that made this a better book:

> Paul Chernoch, Geoffrey Stone, Paul Wonders,
> Ed Pavlik, Christy Pavlik, Abby Pavlik, Georgette Pavlik

Part I — God's Gift

Chapter 1 Beyond Identity

Chapter 2 What Is Identity?

Chapter 3 What Is Reality?

Chapter 4 From Crisis to Crown

Chapter 5 From Desire to Destiny

Chapter 6 Overcome Opposition

Chapter 7 Establish Trust

TO IDENTITY AND BEYOND

The gift of God's son is a gift of eternal life. To know God is to have eternal life. To have eternal life is to have an eternal identity. God wants you to understand who He is and who you are. The devil works to prevent you from discovering your true identity.

Romans 6:23
Isaiah 9:6
Ephesians 2:8–9
John 17:3
John 8:44
Mark 4:15

Chapter 1

Beyond Identity

A young man hurried along the station platform with a thick cardboard mailer under his arm. He didn't know the contents of the package, but he knew its delivery was vital to national security.

The man wore a nondescript, brown delivery shirt and cap; despite frequent glances over his shoulder, he looked like any of the other employees there to assist passengers. But the higher-ups in Washington knew him to be Agent049. Each time he looked back, the two counter-agents trailing him seemed closer; no matter how hard he tried, he just couldn't lose them in the crowd.

Handing off the package to the right person was top priority. But Agent049 had never seen the Agency's East Coast operative. He rehearsed her description.

Tall blond. Early thirties. Tan coat. Red scarf. White gloves.

Two coded questions would verify her identity. *Is this your first trip on the Capitol Limited? Are you headed to Washington on business or pleasure?* The operative would reply, "I'll be visiting my sister Marylyn."

Funny how just a couple of specific questions would be enough to confirm her identity. Her true self was so carefully hidden that only a person armed with the right words could hope to reveal it.

Agent049 took the same precautions, and now it was his turn to become invisible. He slipped around one corner, then another, threw away his cap, put on a pair of glasses, and reversed his shirt to conceal the drab brown and reveal a bright aloha design.

Whatever face Agent049 was wearing on any particular day, that's who the world believed him to be. Some days he would appear as a highly skilled technician or a company representative making his rounds and looking for new clients. At other times he might need to blend fully into the crowd and just look like the guy next door.

Agent049's first few years were exhilarating, but the constant pretending took a toll him. *Why did I ever get into this line of work?* he would ask himself. *I spend so much time in disguise, my alter ego is becoming my reality. I play the part so well that I have lost touch with reality. Who am I deep down inside? Am I even capable of knowing who I really am?*

Like Agent049, we also try on different faces, showing or hiding parts of ourselves to certain people out of fear, or simply because we don't know ourselves. Many people don't know how precious and valuable they are because they're told otherwise by the message of the world. But this book will help you appreciate your true worth by leading you to understand your true identity.

To understand the meaning of your life, you must understand who you are. Moving closer *to* your identity enables you to focus your efforts on your calling *beyond* your identity. You'll discover both who you are (your identity) and why you are (your purpose).

If you had only three more years to live, how would you spend them? Your answer reveals a lot about who you think you are. Would you have fun? Say goodbye? Become sad, depressed, or anxious? Or might you become emboldened to find and live your true purpose? It's amazing how limitations on our time can create urgency and focus.

Jesus had approximately three years from the time He started His ministry until He was crucified. He had a purpose and a strategy for everything He accomplished. He lived up to His identity and fulfilled His deepest longing, and now He calls you to find your passion and advance God's kingdom.

Do you understand how important your identity is to God? You're God's chosen instrument to fulfill His plans. You're irreplaceable. God chooses to exercise His power through His people—and that includes you.

Your contribution is significant—and if you have some doubt about that, this book is for you. These pages will boost your confidence and commitment to God's plan for your life.

You're about to begin an adventure that starts within you, as God reveals who He created you to be. As you see reality from God's perspective and taste His goodness, you're on the path to your true identity. God allows you to look not only with your physical eyes but with His spiritual eyes.

Chapter 1 — Beyond Identity

Fasten your seatbelt; you're about to begin the ride of a lifetime—one that will take you *To Identity and Beyond*.

Play the Long Game

In chess, the pawn is the weakest piece. However, if that's where your understanding of the pawn ends, you'll overlook its potential. If it reaches the other side of the board, it can become the most powerful piece.

I'm not suggesting you play games with your life. Playing the long game means investing the effort necessary to achieve maximum results. Most of the time, this requires sacrificing short-term rewards.

Jesus had a specific purpose for coming to earth. He gave up His earthly life to secure an everlasting victory over death. His life was short in years but long on results. He achieved such outstanding results because He followed the Father's plan. He fulfilled His destiny.

You, too, have a clearly defined destiny. God made you for a specific purpose. Have you invested time into learning what it is?

God wants you to know your identity and walk in good works. The more you know your identity, the more you know your destiny. Your destiny includes what you'll do today and every day of your life.

> *For we are his workmanship, created in Christ Jesus for good works, which God prepared beforehand, that we should walk in them.*
> —Ephesians 2:10

Every moment is an opportunity to prepare for what comes next. In God's economy, nothing you've experienced goes to waste—it always prepares you for the next moment of your life.

You have all you need to reach your potential, but in order to reach it, you must seek and discover. As you become more confident in who God made you to be, you'll see your destination more clearly and be able to accomplish more. But if you don't invest in growth, you delay reaching your potential.

The long-game player finds the optimal balance between immediate satisfaction and maximum impact. Jesus spent time healing people who eventually died. At first glance, this seems like a waste of time. He did it anyway because He cares. He showed us the Father's heart. Jesus excelled at using short-term gains to accomplish God's long-term plans.

You can't play the long game without faith. God alone lives in eternity, seeing your entire life and the end of the world as we know it. Because you can't see that far ahead, you must trust His vision. You can, however, see far enough to take the next step.

Advance God's Kingdom

A believer is God's child and soldier at the same time. As God's spiritual soldier, you advance God's kingdom by knowing your identity and resisting evil.

Jesus advanced God's kingdom, and He left us instructions for how to continue in His absence. Permit me to summarize the Lord's Prayer (Matthew 6:9–13):

> **Father God is perfect. He wants to advance His kingdom on earth. He meets all our needs when we humbly receive His grace and gifts. He meets our physical, emotional, and kingdom desires by His power and for His glory.**

To advance God's kingdom means to expand His reign like yeast expands dough, causing it to rise.[1] When righteousness, peace, and joy increase, the kingdom of God advances (Romans 14:17). The most direct and practical way to advance God's kingdom is to fulfill the Great Commission (Matthew 28:19–20a), the call to all Christians to go into the world and make disciples of all people:

> **Go therefore and make disciples of all nations, baptizing them in the name of the Father and of the Son and of the Holy Spirit, teaching them to observe all that I have commanded you.**

Chapter 1 — Beyond Identity

It's as simple as knowing God and helping others know Him. Just remember: To make a disciple, you first have to be a growing disciple. As a disciple, you allow God to meet your needs through other godly Christians and the help of His Holy Spirit, who is present in the life of every believer.

> *And I will ask the Father, and he will give you another Helper, to be with you forever, even the Spirit of truth, whom the world cannot receive, because it neither sees him nor knows him. You know him, for he dwells with you and will be in you.*
> —John 14:16–17

Enjoy Abundant Life

If you're playing the long game and seeking to advance God's kingdom, He will supply all you need for daily living (Matthew 6:33; Philippians 4:19). And, as a bonus, when you're functioning at your highest level and fulfilling your purpose, you'll experience a joy that satisfies your soul!

Jesus's goal in becoming human, dying, and being resurrected was to bring hope by creating a path to God. Jesus makes it possible for you to move toward the functionality God originally designed for you. He wants you to have life to the fullest.

> *The thief comes only to steal and kill and destroy. I came that they may have life and have it abundantly.*
> —John 10:10

While you're working to advance God's kingdom, the thief works to steal, kill, and destroy your efforts. But you have the Holy Spirit to guide you to all truth (John 16:13), including the truth about your identity, which results in righteousness, peace, and joy.

Study Questions

1. If you only had three more years to live, how would you spend them?
2. What does play the long game mean? How are you doing this now, and what can you do to improve?
3. What does advancing God's kingdom mean to you? How strongly do you desire this?
4. What does having an abundant life mean to you? How satisfied are you with your life?

---

[1] Consider https://www.desiringgod.org/interviews/what-is-the-kingdom-of-god for a more detailed discussion.

Chapter 2

What Is Identity?

Your identity is who you are. More specifically, your identity is who God says you are. Your self-image, who you think or feel you are, is your best understanding of your identity. Here's how they're different.

Identity	Self-Image
Permanent (can't be lost)	Vulnerable (always changing)
Clearly distinct from other people and things	Can be confused with other people and things
Complete	Never has the full picture
Perfectly true and perfectly you	Contains true and false ideas
Intentionally made by God	Made by you but can be influenced by God
Timeless (never changes)	Moves toward or away from identity

You have access to your perfect identity only through your imperfect self-image. Fortunately, because you know you have a true identity, you can continuously self-correct your fragile self-image.

Self-Image Is Vulnerable

In the children's book *Are You My Mother?* by P.D. Eastman, a bird hatches alone and tries to understand who he is. He decides to search for his mother. The baby bird finds and tries out various

potential moms: a kitten, a hen, a dog, a cow, a car, a boat, a plane, and even a power shovel. None of those fits his needs.

Like that bird, you're born lacking understanding and awareness of who you are. Without strong family ties or close friends, you may have a sense of being adrift in life. There is no greater pain than the emptiness and loneliness that results from not knowing who you are, where you are, and to whom you belong.

Only when the bird finds his momma and sees how much he is like her can he experience what it feels like to belong.

After *Who am I?* people typically ask, *What is my purpose for being here?* But to fully answer these questions, you must first ask, *Where did I come from (before this life)?* and *Where am I going (after this life)?*

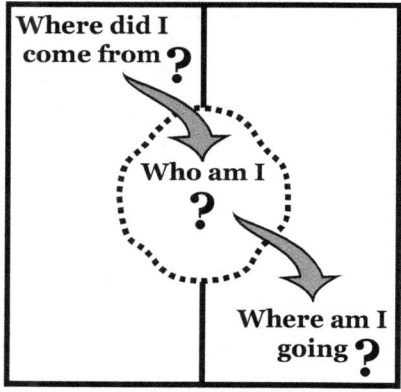

To know who you are, you have to understand your context—where you come from, where you're going, and even who you're not. As explained above, when you're born you're supposed to gain a sense of belonging from your mother. As your awareness develops, so does your scope of belonging. By the time you reach puberty, there are a number of people (or things) that you may depend on as you attempt to find your identity. Consider the following possible contexts you could encounter as you seek an answer to *Who am I?*

- Your parents
- Your friends/peers
- Your church

Chapter 2 — What Is Identity?

- Your government
- Your performance
- Your past
- Your spouse or significant other
- Your child
- The opposite sex
- Your failed relationship(s)
- Your drug of choice (TV, food, sex, pills, alcohol)

Unfortunately, all of these are potentially unreliable sources of a healthy self-image. It gets worse. I need to add one more person to the list: you. How you feel is important information, but it might not accurately represent your identity.

Most people want to be happy. Many people will admit they're living for something outside themselves—their kids, their spouse, their job. Maybe you're living for something, too. The things you live for will influence your self-image. The list is endless, and oftentimes people aren't even aware of how far they've drifted from their true identity. A codependent person may just see herself as sacrificially loving. An alcoholic or workaholic may think he has his impulses under control. A driven athlete may not see her obsession. But our rationalizations don't change the result: we can't help but define ourselves according to our investments.

If you had to define who you are, how good of a job could you do? How self-aware are you?

You start life without any sense of who you are. Your self-image is a blank slate. God provides parents to write truth and love onto you. You need a family to help you learn who you are. If you lack a family, you miss the foundation of meaning and identity. But as important as family is, it's never enough.

Every person has a God-shaped hole in their heart that is too big for anyone else to fill. Successful parents step aside at the right time, allowing God to fill His rightful place.

Whether you believe in God or not, your purpose will remain hidden and unrealizable without God's presence in your life. Nature abhors a vacuum, so you will find yourself under intense pressure to supplement your identity with one thing or another.

You'll wander aimlessly through life, like that bird, until you accept your God-given identity.

In the *Star Wars* movies, it was foretold that Anakin Skywalker would bring "balance to the Force"—a mystical power accessible to certain heroes and villains in that universe. And indeed, throughout these movies, he is trying to figure out which side is which. He doesn't know where he belongs. He doesn't have a biological father, and this leaves him vulnerable to looking in the wrong places for his identity.

At first, he seems like he is going to be okay. As a child, he has good mentors and identifies with their peaceful cause. But as a teenager, he is drawn to the dark side. He lets the evil emperor mentor him and dictate who he will become: Darth Vader.

The idea of acquiring behavioral characteristics of the one we follow is called imprinting. This occurs when we model the behavior of our closest relation. Imprinting is most obvious in young animals, such as ducklings, who follow their mother around in order to learn the basics of being a duck.

Animals are imprinted. Human children are parented. Adults are mentored. Imprinting, parenting, and mentoring are all important but temporary phases. Eventually, the beginner needs to separate from his mentor so he can function independently with his own identity.

Asking *Who am I?* is important. However, if you don't know to whom you belong, you're going to end up more confused than before you asked. Asking the right person will yield the right answer. For example, God can speak through someone close to you—perhaps your mother. Her answer to your question *Who am I?* is "You're loved." But asking the wrong person will yield a wrong answer. For example, a codependent woman might ask her abusive husband who she is. His answer: "You're worthless."

Identity Is Permanent

You have an identity, but do you know what it is and how to use it as God intended? God is the keeper of your true identity, and He made it to be as unchanging and eternal as He is.

Chapter 2 — What Is Identity?

The spiritually regenerated human has the most potential out of all of creation. Your identity is your most valuable possession, and yet you might not be aware of its existence.

Do you know why you make the decisions you do? Are you motivated by selfish desires or a need to please someone else? Or are you living based on who God made you to be?

Are you sure?

Identity is just as real as gravity, a force that affects your life whether you understand it or not. But once gravity is understood, all kinds of air and space travel become possible.

Consider what may become possible in your own life once you gain an understanding of who God made you to be.

God knows everything about you, including the parts you have yet to discover. Your self-image is a mixture of true and false self-beliefs you've acquired over the years. So much in life can confuse your self-image when you don't know your true identity.

All you know about yourself, all you've forgotten, and all you have never known—these all shape your everyday decisions. That's why it's important to understand everything that drives your behavior.

Knowing who you really are may feel impossible, and in one sense it is. Only God knows you completely; He'll always know you better than you know yourself. But don't let this stop you from growing your self-image ever closer to your identity.

Seeking out who you are takes time. It requires exploring your thoughts, feelings, and experiences. When you buy a complicated appliance or tool, it's important to read the instructions. Likewise, using talents and gifts the right way is impossible without first discovering their purpose. The effort is always worth it. Once you know who God made you to be, you don't want to be anyone else.

If you want to know what drives your behaviors, you must make a conscious effort because God has strategically hidden who you are. Who you are in God's eyes—your true identity—won't be obvious for at least three reasons:

1. God created you to develop over time. You need a variety of experiences to prove who you are.
2. Your spiritual identity can only be revealed by God in His time.
3. The experiences you have can provide false (or misleading) ideas that distort instead of clarify who you are.

We have looked at identity as who you are. The dictionary also defines identity as "the set of characteristics by which you're definitively recognizable." This confirms your uniqueness and that your *identity* distinguishes you from others. Your identity is also "what remains the same, constant, and persisting over time, under varying circumstances." This definition provides the insight that *identity* must be permanently yours.

If your identity is your set of characteristics that never change, then they must have come from the one who created you. If you want to know who you are, you have to ask your Heavenly Father. He is your point of origin, your starting place. Before you physically existed, you existed as an idea in God's creative mind. You came from God and one day you will return to God. In the meantime, God is with you by His Holy Spirit.

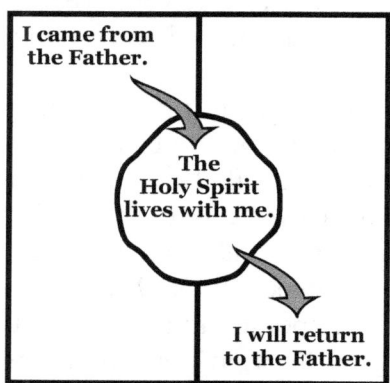

God has gifted you with a true identity. All those things I mentioned before—parents, friends, church, career, spouse, kids, possessions—might seem to give you an identity, but if you want to know who you truly are, you must seek God.

God makes each person in His image. Each person is one of a kind, sufficiently intricate and distinct from every other person.

Chapter 2 — What Is Identity?

Assigned the same task, we will all approach it differently. God created you with an intentional design and therefore an intentional purpose. He made you to last forever (not in your current body, but in spirit).

God knows everything there is to know about you.

Your eyes saw my unformed body;
all the days ordained for me
were written in your book
before one of them came to be.
—Psalm 139:16

If you want to know your identity, God is the only one who can give you an authoritative, definitive answer. God's Spirit and His Bible are the only completely reliable sources that help you discern between truth-reinforcing experiences and lie-reinforcing experiences. All other sources will mislead you to some degree. Not that you shouldn't ask. Others people can be aware of certain pieces of your identity, and God can use them to deliver His message to you.

Knowledge of self and God go hand in hand. You can't know one without the other. Knowing God helps you know yourself better; knowing yourself better helps you know God better. The closer you are to who God made you to be, the closer you'll be to God. True self-intimacy produces intimacy with God. You can't learn about yourself without also learning about God.

Know God   **Know Self**

God wants you to know both who He is and who you are. How could God create you with intention, but then not want to lead, guide, and communicate with you? God is on your side. What could be better than God allowing you to see His plan for your life?

Identity Has Purpose

Your identity is inseparable from your purpose. If God intentionally created you as distinct from others, your uniqueness must have a purpose. While you can't expect to discover your purpose overnight, you can be sure you have one at all times.

Claim and Discover Your Identity

God has given you your identity as a loving gift. Claim it by acknowledging that you have an identity beyond your self-image.

Discovering who you are is a key secret to enjoying life. As a Christian, you're priceless, one of a kind, and irreplaceable; you're essential to God's plans. Every Christian is important, but too few people make the effort to find out *how* they are important.

Who am I? Doesn't everyone long to know the answer to this question? Yes and no. Yes, we want to know the truth. We have a built-in desire to be recognized and to be significant. And yet we fear making contact with the lies we believe about ourselves because of the shame and pain we believe we deserve. Instead of confronting these lies and the feelings they evoke, we attempt to bury it all as deep as we can.

You're on a quest for the buried treasure that is *you*. God buried who you are within yourself.

When you dig for treasure, expect that you'll have to sort through a lot of junk. Dig anyway.

You can't choose your identity. A person who tries to make up her identity puts on a mask like an actor. Instead, you can only discover the identity God has already planned and created. You live in the context of a story greater than yourself. God wants you to dig, as if for a treasure, to uncover your part in His story. Seek for the truth, He says, and you will find it; knock and the door will be opened (Matthew 7:7).

To understand yourself completely, you need both a deep internal understanding of yourself and an extensive understanding of God and the rest of creation. To gain a healthy self-image, pursue these four areas of your life:

Chapter 2 — What Is Identity?

1. **Social relationships:** You're able to give and receive love. You appreciate others' strengths and know how you can help compliment their weaknesses.
2. **Skills to use in the world:** You can understand creation and how you can contribute according to the ways God made you. This includes your achievements and mastery.
3. **Self-awareness:** You can understand your identity apart from your accomplishments. You feel a strong sense of worth; you know why God created you.
4. **Spiritual connection to God:** You continue to grow in your understanding of God's grace and truth as demonstrated by Jesus. You can join with the Holy Spirit to accomplish God's plans for your life.

Would you like to experience joy and get what you want from life? Then set a goal to maximize the truth and minimize the false ideas about who you are. Maximize your potential by discovering who you are. Seek and accept who God made you to be. Your joy increases as you grow in the knowledge and acceptance of your God-given identity.

Claim and Discover Your Destiny

Destiny[2] follows identity. Claim your destiny by recognizing you have a purpose because of your identity. If you know your identity, then you will know your purpose. If you don't know your purpose, then you must not know your identity all that well.

Your Father planned a path for you. You started as an idea in God's mind and went through spiritual death and physical birth. When you become a Christian, you experience spiritual birth and gain access to your identity in Christ. God made you in His image, yet unique; therefore, you display His image in ways no one else can. You're spiritually alive, but you can still wander from the truth. Despite your imperfect journey, because God predestined you to be conformed to His image, you're on a path of destiny (Romans 8:29).

When you look at the long-term trajectory of your path, you'll see your self-image is consistently moving closer to your true identity.

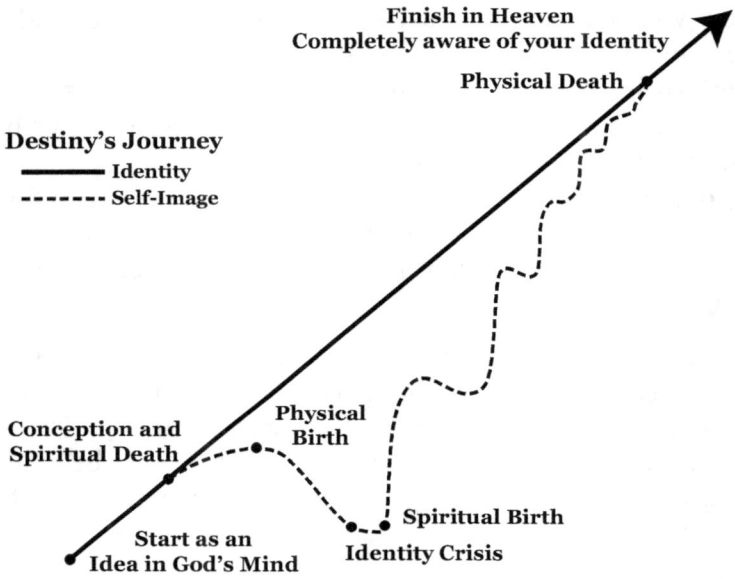

When you're born, at first you're unable to know who you are. You learn who you are implicitly by what you experience. As a young child, your focus shifts as you explore the ways in which you can change your external world. Then during adolescence, you become aware of your internal thought life. However, only when you become born again spiritually will you be able to resist the pull of the vacuum and join with God to fulfill His purposes.

During your life journey, you encounter various experiences and spiritual forces. The good forces guide you to the truth; the evil forces attempt to hide the truth from you and sell you lies. You'll inevitably believe some of those lies are true.

When you consistently ask the wrong people to define you or chase after the wrong things for fulfillment, this will take a toll. The detour can take you far away from the path God has intended. Depending upon the severity and the degree of falsehood you've experienced and believed, you might have a lot of false identity to unlearn. Fortunately, you don't have to relearn the truth about yourself that you've already come to know.

God doesn't want you to feel negative and defeated. But He understands why you would feel that way. The good news is, when you finally cast off what is false, you'll be stronger than ever before. The process of refuting the lies and embracing the truth brings you closer to God.

As you gain a true connection with your Creator, you'll realize the intentions of your design. You can participate in the true inside-out growth of your self-image because God's Holy Spirit lives within you. His presence relieves the pressure to fill the vacuum from the outside-in. But you still have to grow one day at a time. You'll need to exercise patience as you see to your daily tasks and wait for God to unfold the full details of your destiny in His timing.

Take heart—God is in control. God cares about the smallest details of everyday life, but doesn't allow them to interfere with the more important spiritual goals. God wants you to seek life's blessings, but He also wants you to defer your desires to the bigger picture of what He has planned for your life.

The Lord Almighty created you for a real, specific purpose, and He is determined to bring it to fruition. He is faithful to finish what He started (Philippians 1:6). You have a purpose, predetermined by the Lord. His purposes for your life are greater than you know. It's time to affirm your destiny.

In the next couple of chapters, let's look at the catalysts for change, the factors that drive us to embrace our God-given identity and destiny.

Study Questions

1. What is the difference between self-image and identity?
2. What would your life be like if you had a self-image but no God-given identity?
3. In your search for belonging, what people or things have you tried before you found God? When you asked, *Who am I?* what kind of answers did you receive?
4. Do you know for sure where you've come from and where you're going?
5. What does it mean to you that you were an idea in God's mind before you were born?
6. How close do you believe your self-image is to your identity?
7. How spiritually self-aware do you think you are?
8. What are some lies you believe about yourself?
9. What are some lies you tell about yourself?
10. Who are you?

Seek out the help of pastors, friends, family, and other spiritually mature people. Have them help you discover more about yourself by completing a Johari Window. This is a quadrant designed by psychologists in the 1950s to help people better understand themselves and their relationships with others.[3] Are you surprised by what you know and don't know about yourself? Take your findings to God. Ask Him to reveal your identity. Remember, only God knows your complete identity.

---

[2] Destiny is both an inevitable series of events (as in God knows it completely and predestined your path) and your future that you can pursue (as in something you don't know completely and must walk out in faith as you learn your identity). Keep both in mind throughout this book.
[3] See https://en.wikipedia.org/wiki/Johari_window

Chapter 3

What Is Reality?

In Chapter 2, you learned that you need a context to understand identity. Reality is the ultimate context because it includes everything. Reality starts with God. He's the only one who completely understands reality. More specifically, God's existence defines reality.

Your worldview is your set of deeply held beliefs that determine your approach to life and provide a context for your self-image. Your worldview is what you believe about reality, just as your self-image is what you believe about your identity.

Reality	Worldview
Objective; God defines	Subjective; you define
God and His creation	Your mind and its perceptions
Real, actual, biblical	Contains distortions
Includes everything	Never has the full picture
Timeless (never changes)	Moves toward or away from reality

Learning your worldview is essential because self-image and worldview influence each other for better or worse. For example, if you believe you're unlovable, you'll likely project this onto God by believing He is unloving. Furthermore, a poor self-image is hurtful to you, but an inaccurate worldview has the potential to hurt others. What would happen if you shared the following worldview with everyone you meet? *God doesn't love any of us; you can't trust Him.*

In the 2004 *Battlestar Galactica* reboot, the technology exists to create robots that not only look human but also fully believe they are human. For these robots, being human was their perceived reality even though it wasn't true.

Maybe the world as you know it doesn't match up with reality. Do you trust your perception of the experiences you have each day?

TO IDENTITY AND BEYOND

We perceive only what our senses tell our brains. Some argue there is no objective reality because all observers only process sensations according to their subjective perceptions. In other words, if a tree falls in a forest and no one is around, does it make a sound? If there is no instrument to receive the sound, is there really an audible sound?

For humans, our perception is what we call reality, but this isn't necessarily God's reality. We can live a lie fully believing it's true.

Maybe reality is like a dream—a product of your imagination that only you experience. In the movie *The Matrix,* most people are born into a virtual reality while being unaware of their physical reality. They think they're free but are really imprisoned and manipulated by an artificial intelligence (AI). Chillingly, the AI configured the fake reality to look like our everyday lives (with sights, sounds, homes, jobs, relationships, etc.). The reality we all know would make an efficient mental prison. But this is only because God hard-wired us to comprehend it.

These movies question the very fabric of reality. What if reality isn't what you think it is? What if it's significantly better or worse than you thought? What if you found out you aren't who you thought you were? What if you're really a robot? How do you know you're not part of an alien species? Can you know for sure who you are?

Soren Kierkegaard (1813–1855) is considered the father of existentialism, which is the study of human existence. A Christian, Kierkegaard believed that, "truth is subjectivity and subjectivity is truth." This wasn't a belief in relativism—the idea that truth changes from person to person. Instead, it was his way of saying truth is more than intellectual knowledge—each person must apply the truth to his heart. Truth doesn't do anyone any lasting good unless it's personal. As Kierkegaard sought to know reality, he questioned his context:

Where am I? Who am I?
How did I come to be here?
What is this thing called the world?
How did I come into the world?
Why was I not consulted?

Chapter 3 — What Is Reality?

*And if I am compelled to take part in it,
where is the director? I want to see him.*
—Soren Kierkegaard

To understand your existence, you must discover what is real. Reality is the absence of deception and denial. When you see the reality of something, you see it as it really is.

What do you believe about reality? How each person defines his worldview is entirely up to that individual. Many people create a worldview that supports their experiences without considering God's truth. They make up their own truth by creating beliefs that aren't true, or by cherry-picking some truths while ignoring others.

Your worldview can limit your self-image. For example, you could believe everyone can create their own identity. But trying to develop a genuine weakness into a strength wastes time. Not believing in God also has an impact on self-image. If you don't have a creator to determine your value, what will?

Are you needed, wanted, and loved? Do you fit anywhere? Does your existence have significance? Are your talents needed, or are they redundant, serving no real purpose? Are you a decoration, or are you essential? Optional or required? Irrelevant or indispensable?

Your worldview is your best understanding of the meaning of life. Are you here by aimless, random chance? Or did God intentionally create *you* for a purpose? Are you merely an animal, or are you a child of God—made in God's image?

Your perception is your reality, but it may or may not be God's reality. You must live with your perceptions, even when they aren't true. Whether you believe God exists or not, you have some belief about God. Is God in control of what happens? Does God care about you? Your attitude toward God creates deeply held convictions about the world in which you live. Are you indifferent toward God? Antagonistic? Allied? Doubtful?

Let's examine four worldviews that are commonly held today.

<u>Naturalism</u>

Naturalism emphasizes science by focusing on creation as discoverable. Science defines *real* as whatever is repeatable, observable, and measurable. Science downplays or flat-out ignores the spiritual or whatever it can't explain, leaving its focus on external reality. Science omits anything not observable by senses (or an instrument that bridges the gap between a physical reality and our senses).

Biblical objections: Christians believe a spiritual reality is as real as our physical reality. Scientific methods are significant, but they're incomplete as a worldview because they deny a spiritual reality. At best, this worldview explains one half of reality. At worst, it misrepresents reality.[4]

Relativism

Relativism is just the opposite of naturalism. It says each individual decides in her own mind what is real. Whatever she believes or perceives is true, that is her truth, and there can be no other objective truth. An extreme belief in relativism might lead a person to argue that nothing physical exists. Choices don't make any significant difference because everything is relative. Reality is impossible to define because it is constantly evolving. It is malleable and can change into anything at any given moment.

Any subjective reality you can create, even if pure fantasy, is accepted. This worldview promotes the idea that "you can be anything you want." Reality is what you interpret it to be.

Biblical objections: The Bible doesn't teach that you can be anything you want, but you can be more of who God made you to be. Relativism is incomplete because it denies the objective reality God has created. If you form a relativistic worldview, you're in danger of losing sight of who God is and what He has intended for you.

Humanism

Humanism says humans are capable beings and don't require help from God. This worldview doesn't necessarily deny the existence of both an objective physical reality and a spiritual reality, but argues that religions are manmade. If God exists, surely humans can work or perform their way to God. Everyone must keep score, and individual performance will determine how blessed or poor the next life will be.

Biblical objections: Christians believe reality is created by God. Only a prideful person would believe he's capable enough or good enough to make life work under his own efforts. The truth is that we all fall short, and no amount of religious effort will propel us forward in the afterlife.

Only the Christian faith has a unique, non-works worldview that is also backed by historical evidence and the Bible.

Christianity

In a Christian worldview, God is the objective constant. He is a permanent observer of all of creation. God is the one true objective reality. Everything else must be defined in relation to Him.

Christians rely on the Bible and the Holy Spirit as absolute truth. The Bible explains God as a trinity—three persons in one—the Father, the Son, and the Holy Spirit. To be a Christian, you must believe that the Father sent His Son Jesus to save you from your sin by His death and resurrection. Jesus says He is the way, the truth, and the life. The Holy Spirit is the helper who dwells with all believers to guide them into truth (John 14:6, 16, 17, 26).

> *"I will not leave you as orphans, I will come to you. Yet a little while and the world will see me no more, but you will see me. Because I live, you also will live. In that day you will know that I am in my Father, and you in me, and I in you."*
> —John 14:18–20
>
> *I have been crucified with Christ. It is no longer I who live, but Christ who lives in me. And the life I now live in the flesh I live by faith in the Son of God, who loved me and gave himself for me.*
> —Galatians 2:20

When you become a Christian, you're no longer spiritually dead. Christ lives inside you making you spiritually alive, similar to how a battery powers a phone. The Holy Spirit is an intimate power source, enabling you to enjoy open fellowship with God. God makes you His home and comes to live with you.

A Christian worldview assumes the following:
- God exists as Creator-Father, and He is separate from and in complete control of His creation.
- God brings order, value, and purpose to His creation. He separates and makes distinction while creating. He also maintains unity and oneness against the onslaught of chaos and disorder.
- You're part of creation, but you're also separate from God and the rest of creation.
- You have an identity; you're unique, and God has made you for a specific purpose.
- God is spirit, and because He created you in His image, you also have a spirit. A spiritual reality exists along with a physical reality.
- Only God knows everything; our reality contains mysteries and unknowns.

What Is God's Reality?

God defines reality by who He is. Jesus is the truth. To see Jesus is to see the truest reality. Without God, reality wouldn't exist. As hard as it is to understand that God has always existed, it's harder to imagine an existence of nothing.

Creation is the part of reality that God made through Jesus in the presence of His Holy Spirit. God sustains creation by His power

God's Reality

God	Creation
	(Your Identity)

(Hebrews 1:2–3). So, your identity is part of creation, which is part of God's reality. God gives you the freedom to embrace or reject reality, but that doesn't make it any less real.

God and His reality are fixed. However, your perception of God's reality will change according to your experiences and maturity level. You view God and creation via the lens of your self-image. Unfortunately, the lens collects dust (false beliefs) that distorts your worldview. No two people see the world the same way.

Your Reality, Perceptions, Worldview

God-View	Interpretation of Experiences
	Self-Image

Creation is a significant part of God's reality. The other part is spiritual, which bridges the gulf between physical reality and God (1 Corinthians 2:6–16). God is spirit. Without the spiritual reality, we would have no concept or awareness of God. You must be born again spiritually to establish a connection with God and see His reality.

Reality Is Inescapable

God created everything and controls everything, no matter what you believe. This objective reality is inescapable. Every experience you have within this reality will make an impact on you, for better or worse. God brought you into a world that is already up and running. You entered the world mid-story.

God chooses the time and place you're born, your gender, your parents, and even your entire identity (Acts 17:26). He controls everything. In this respect, you're more like a goldfish in a bowl than a shark in an infinitely expansive ocean. Your job is one of discovery, not creation of a new self or a new world. God means for you to utilize what He provides, not usurp the life He designed by transforming it into something no longer recognizable as God's.

You may be thinking, *Wow! My life is dependent on someone more powerful than me holding everything together.* It gets better.

Not only has God created and defined the reality we were born into, He also programmed into us how to discern the beauty of that reality. Sure, everybody has different preferences, but we can't escape our inherent sense of what is awe-inspiringly beautiful. No one will say a colorful sunset, a vast canyon, or a bubbling brook is ugly. That is, unless they're in outright rebellion to God and favor death, deceit, destruction, and labeling black as white and white as black. Some people will try to paint over God's original work and create a counterfeit reality. That is what evil does. But counterfeit creations will quickly fade out of existence, much like how paint wears away, exposing natural wood underneath.

Reality Is Unchangeable

God's reality is inescapable *and* unchangeable. Only God can create something completely original, inject something new into reality, or make a fundamental change to reality. The basic framework of the universe is stable. There's nothing new under the sun. God doesn't change. All ideas come from God first.

An artist can create something new, but only within the bounds of what God supplies. An artist is able to influence how a painting looks by choosing which colors to use and how to mix them on a canvas, but God provides the canvas, the paint, the colors, the ability to see, an appreciation for color, the skill to paint, and inspiration through His creation. You just can't escape His dominion. God makes the rules, not you—but you have choices to make within God's reality.

You participate in reality in the same way that a child plays with Legos. God provides an abundance of colors, shapes, and sizes. You can create with them, but you don't have the power to add new bricks. Yes, you can alter or destroy some aspects of creation, but you can't change the underlying structure of reality. God already decided how reality works. He's woven His very nature into the fabric of creation. For example, no one would say stealing is good (at least not if they're the one being stolen from). Everyone has an imprint of right and wrong on their heart.

Every story ever written is ultimately about God's reality. Your life is a story of discovery, redemption, and becoming who God made you to be. You can't create your identity. Your identity isn't a blank slate; God created your DNA that determines who you are.

Reality Is Experiential

You can't change God's reality, but you can explore, discover, and rearrange it. You learn about this inescapable and unchangeable reality through your experiences. Experiences lead you to form beliefs. These beliefs can be true (in alignment with God's reality) or false (out of alignment with God's reality). The goal is to examine your beliefs and then embrace the truth and reject the lies.

God gives us senses, language, and experiences to encourage external exploration. And God gives us His Holy Spirit to encourage an internal validation of external experiences. Therefore, you can double-check your perceptions. You need all the input God provides in order to make an informed decision about God's reality.

While we all start off life without any preconceived notions of the world, no one can stay that way for long. Your life experiences immediately begin to shape your self-image. At first, every interaction with the world happens alongside your immediate family, and so they directly affect your beliefs. As you get older, you start to encounter other people and these outside influences reshape your worldview. How you interpret your experiences will move you toward or away from the truth.

Much like in the movie *The Matrix*, there are false realities that you can cling to, and then there is the true reality, God's reality, from which you'll never be able to escape.

God structured the universe so that all its parts fit together. He created us to desire good things and to know when we're experiencing good or evil. He gives us a nervous system that registers pain. He created sound, and He created ears that can hear the sounds. So even a fake, virtual reality must be compatible with our built-in hardware—our brains. God hardwired us to fit only within the reality He created.

You need to taste and see for yourself. Solomon tasted many royal luxuries and resolved that although life is good, he couldn't fill his deepest longings with creation (Ecclesiastes 1:12–2:16). When you consider only what is available to your five senses (naturalism), you deprive yourself of spiritual fulfillment. Keep your eyes open to spiritual reality. See with your heart (the mystery), not just your head (the facts). Consider the Creator behind the creation that you enjoy.

You're part of creation, so you're discoverable just like the rest of creation. You're not something that evolves randomly by chance. You can't create your own destiny. To fear God is to respect the mysterious aspect of God and creation.

Reality Is Mysterious

God's reality is here whether we like it or not. It's inescapable. Only God knows everything. All aspects of reality are mysterious until we manage to discover them, one by one. There is so much we don't know. We could discover something new about creation every day.

Consider this: Of the fifty greatest discoveries that changed the world, 74 percent happened within the last three hundred years.[5] We still discover thousands of new species every year. And with all of our advancements in neuroscience, still we know only a fraction of what there is to know about the brain. Life is full of mystery and unknowns. And God is the keeper if it all.

God can't be surprised by a new discovery. For God, there's nothing new to discover. But there is one experience He is waiting to have. His frontier lies within the human heart. You're in control of how much you open your heart to Him. He eagerly anticipates each moment you learn a new truth about Him or yourself, His child.

There are so many lies and misconceptions to filter out, but God's appetite for revelation should give you hope. If you can grasp who God is through Jesus Christ and the Holy Spirit, then you can also grasp who you are. On some level, all of life is faith because you must engage in the process of discovery all along the way. Only God knows all the missing pieces to who you are. Ask God, and He

Chapter 3 — What Is Reality?

will reveal what you need to know about your identity. When part of you remains hidden, trust God with the mystery.

As you see reality from God's perspective and taste His goodness, you're on the path to your true identity. God allows you to look not only with your physical eyes but with His spiritual eyes.

God gives the ability to see some of reality to all believers. He keeps His secrets hidden and reveals them only to His children. He provides information to everyone, but He only grants understanding to those whom He chooses (Matthew 16:17, 13:10–17). Even His children must seek after spiritual understanding. But being able, through faith, to see God's deeper truths makes all the difference. Reality is that important.

Reality Is Broken

God's original plan for life was pain-free. Sin led to the Fall, which brought the curse of death and pain. Suffering is a part of everyone's reality.

How you understand suffering is part of your worldview. Which of the following scenarios best describes your perspective?
1. Life is a place like heaven where needs are mostly met and there is little suffering (evil doesn't exist).
2. Life is a place like hell where needs are rarely met and suffering and isolation are constant companions (God doesn't exist).
3. Life is a place with aspects of both heaven and hell.

If you select scenario 1, you'll expect that you shouldn't ever suffer, believing that any suffering is injustice. You'll believe that given enough time, humans can perfect the world they live in and have an approximation of heaven on earth. You'll minimize and deny evil's influence. Consequently, you might start to emphasize life on earth more than eternal life in heaven.

If you select scenario 2, you'll minimize God's power, believing He is impotent. You'll work to make sure others won't get the best of you, and you'll attempt to enjoy what you can from life. When this fails, you'll become bitter and angry and probably give up on

God. You'll live with constant disappointment in God because He refuses to eliminate all suffering. Consequently, feeling hopeless, you might turn away from God.

If you select scenario 3, you'll be set up for optimal success. You'll expect that God is reachable and willing to help you, and you'll be able to grow in spite of the cruelties found in the world. You'll expect times of suffering. You'll realize you suffer as part of God's plan, but you'll groan for heaven. You'll participate in suffering instead of violently protesting it like a victim. You'll suffer honorably, as Jesus did, realizing God allows it for His purpose.

Strangely enough, scenarios 1 and 2 have a lot in common. Both require distorting who God is to make them work. Both ultimately result in disappointment. Life is clearly not the paradise God originally planned.

So how can you endure in a world where evil and a perfectly loving God coexist? Such a reality requires hard work. There's little room to take a breather. Life is a short-lived burden—an aching to move beyond its childbirth pains (Romans 8:22). Life is also an incredible gift—an opportunity to experience waking up from a false reality and discovering God's goodness.

Consider this life a trial in which you can choose your destination. You have access to God, but some suffering is unavoidable. Sometimes you have access to people, and other times you experience isolation. You can grow closer to God, but your view of reality is clouded (1 Corinthians 13:12).

So don't settle for passive indifference. You must either deny or accept reality. Face your experiences and reconcile them with what the Bible says about God. If you push hard enough, you'll understand God made life for you to discover, not redefine. If you persist in asking God to reveal His glory, He will eventually do so (Exodus 33:18–23).

Everyone has a worldview just as everyone has a self-image. Instead of settling for worldly wisdom that comes from the despair of this life, be intentional about defining your convictions based on God's wisdom (see 1 Corinthians 1:18–31).

Chapter 3 — What Is Reality?

    A worldview is like a map. When you're lost in the woods, a map helps you know where you are in relation to where you want to be. Knowing reality is a matter of life and death. Like a map, a worldview is only as useful as it is accurate.

    Your worldview is a set of beliefs that help you see a way forward in the darkest night. When evil comes to confuse your way, you'll have an answer prepared (1 Peter 3:15). You won't have to endure the terror of being lost (Ephesians 4:14). You'll know your way home. You can be hopeful even while you suffer.

Study Questions

1. How do you feel about reality being inescapable? Unchangeable? Mysterious? Broken?
2. How excited are you to discover more about God, creation, and your identity?
3. How difficult is it for you to believe God is good in a world where evil and suffering are common occurrences?
4. Read 1 Corinthians 1:18–31. What is true wisdom?
5. Do you agree with the definition of God's reality as described by the Christian worldview? What do you believe about reality? How have your experiences influenced your worldview? Write down your worldview.

---

[4] https://www.nybooks.com/articles/1997/01/09/billions-and-billions-of-demons. Professor Richard Lewontin: We take the side of science in spite of the patent absurdity of some of its constructs, in spite of its failure to fulfill many of its extravagant promises of health and life, in spite of the tolerance of the scientific community for unsubstantiated just-so stories, because we have a prior commitment, a commitment to materialism. … we cannot allow a Divine Foot in the door.

[5] For example, see https://www.theatlantic.com/magazine/archive/2013/11/innovations-list/309536

Chapter 4

From Crisis to Crown

In the movie *The Two Towers*, the evil wizard Saruman is building an army big enough to snuff out all that is good. Merry, a Hobbit, realizing the world is in danger, seeks the help of Treebeard the Ent, guardian of the forest. Merry pleads, "You must help. Please. You must do something." After significant delays, Merry's friend Pippin, also a Hobbit, sends Treebeard to a vantage point where he can see the devastation first-hand. Saruman is cutting down and burning Treebeard's forest to fuel his army. Upon seeing all the downed trees, Treebeard exclaims, "Many of these trees were my friends. Creatures I had known from nut and acorn." Rather than bemoan their fate, Treebeard rallies the other Ents and determines to go to war.

Just prior to the encounter with Treebeard, Pippin is tempted to give up the fight against evil and return home. But Merry reminds Pippin that if they don't do something, "There won't be a Shire."

Moments of crisis help you determine what really matters in life. You, too, should look for the turning points in your life when a fire awakens in your soul. *I have to do something!* What will cause you to take action? If you're in denial of the reality of evil, you'll retreat to your life comforts, believing evil won't reach that far. You must see the reality of evil to be motivated to take action. Then you'll rise in spiritual power to bring about change that brings glory to God.

Stepping forward in faith means taking action. This may entail acting upon the world or upon your own heart. You may need to step up your activity or relinquish your control. Either approach can be a faithful response depending upon your heart, your circumstances, and God's leading.

Differentiating between faith and foolish abandon is essential. Because a crisis is first of all spiritual, don't act without the Lord's presence alongside you. The Lord invites you to trust and rest while you wait for His timing. The might of your physical actions doesn't compare to the might of the Lord's presence. Let the Lord Almighty do the heavy lifting. You honor the Lord by deferring to His strength and initiative. Be like Merry and Pippin who persistently waited for the physically stronger Treebeard.

A huge crisis can dramatically change your life: divorce, bankruptcy, betrayal, life-threatening illness, or losing a loved one. Even a minor crisis can be life altering: being unhappy in your career, marital conflict, financial setbacks, disobedient children, or being fired. A crisis will only influence your self-image if you let it. What happens to you is beyond your control, but your response has consequences.

How you respond to events impacts your well-being. Whether you become discouraged or stay positive when bad things happen, the crisis can help you find your way toward deeper understanding. If you respond poorly, your self-image will suffer, and you might lose touch with who you really are. Big crises can shake you to your core and lead you to question who you are.

An identity crisis is more than a physical problem; it's a spiritual problem that requires a spiritual solution. A lot is at risk. Your response affects not only your life but also the expansion of God's kingdom.

Identity Crisis

A crisis is an opportunity to learn who you really are. When circumstances are against you and despair wraps around your neck, look inward for God's reality. What is God doing in your life? What is He saying? Are you allowing Him to strengthen and energize your heart?

Losing a friend is heartbreaking. Sometimes this cup is bittersweet, like when your best friend moves away to college. Or it can be spiked with poison. Imagine a best friend stealing the love of your life. The shock of betrayal would gut you. Yet in the midst of your heartache, however bitter the circumstance, you can come away with a stronger understanding of what it means to be a friend.

Or what if you're the selfish one? What if you backstabbed your friend? Living with the shame of a foolish decision can be

Chapter 4 — From Crisis to Crown

devastating. You might give up on yourself—or you could find hope to move forward.

The benefit of a crisis is the opportunity to grow. If you forfeit that opportunity, you only reap the negatives. But on the positive side, a crisis can

- interrupt what you consider to be important,
- highlight that you're stuck and your life is on hold,
- expose cancerous sin in your heart that needs to go,
- agitate the status quo to force you to decide how to move forward in life,
- call you deeper to find the meaning of life and pursue healthy desires,
- encourage connection with God through grief and lament,
- confront your false beliefs and confirm and strengthen truth in your heart,
- clarify your priorities and values—what really matters, and
- transform you into a better version of yourself.

When you respond positively to a crisis, your self-image becomes closer to your perfect and complete identity. God calls a struggle during a crisis a trial. He says to expect trials and suffering (Romans 5:3, John 16:33); you're to embrace them because they're good for strengthening your faith. And, as a bonus, you'll receive a crown!

> *Count it all joy, my brothers, when you meet trials of various kinds, for you know that the testing of your faith produces steadfastness. And let steadfastness have its full effect, that you may be perfect and complete, lacking in nothing. Blessed is the man who remains steadfast under trial, for when he has stood the test he will receive the crown of life, which God has promised to those who love him.*
> —James 1:2–4, 12

TO IDENTITY AND BEYOND

A crisis turns up the heat on your life, revealing the weakness in your worldview. You may question God: *Are You for me or against me? Did you make me treasure or junk? Am I valuable or worthless?* First assess the damage, then formulate a better worldview. Maybe all you need is to strengthen what you already know. Maybe you need to replace a few faulty ideas. Or maybe you need a complete overhaul. Which is it? When you aren't sure, that's an identity crisis.

Like a rite of passage, identity crises will come. On the journey to adulthood, everyone must navigate being misunderstood or rejected by peers, adults, and the opposite sex. Many only find safe passage much later in life. But it doesn't have to be that way.

Growth requires a challenge, just like a weight lifter needs resistance to grow his muscles. Stress applied to muscles prompts the body to work to increase muscle mass. Dealing with a crisis is as hard as pumping iron, but each serves a purpose. When you're too weak to face life's challenges, you need endurance. But you can be hopeful even while you're fatigued because you know your muscles are growing stronger.

An identity crisis happens when you realize you don't have enough figured out about life and your place in the world. When you can't meet the demands of life. When life doesn't work. These are all signals that you need to grow.

Difficult circumstances leave you no choice but to move away from neutral. Your current model breaks when you encounter exceptional life experiences. If you've been avoiding the stakes, they've just been raised. Your current worldview is no longer an accurate model for reality.

Your life satisfaction isn't limited by other people or your circumstances. Your main source of unhappiness isn't people who have failed you, it is failing to grasp all of who God made you to be. A sour attitude can block you from seeing your identity.

The biggest crisis you'll ever face is realizing that nothing in creation can completely satisfy you. Your flesh[6] will be insatiable until you get to heaven (see Ecclesiastes 5:8–20; 6:7).

An existential crisis demands a transition. When a crisis hits, you have two directions in which you can go:

1. Distrust and move away from God.
2. Trust and move toward God.

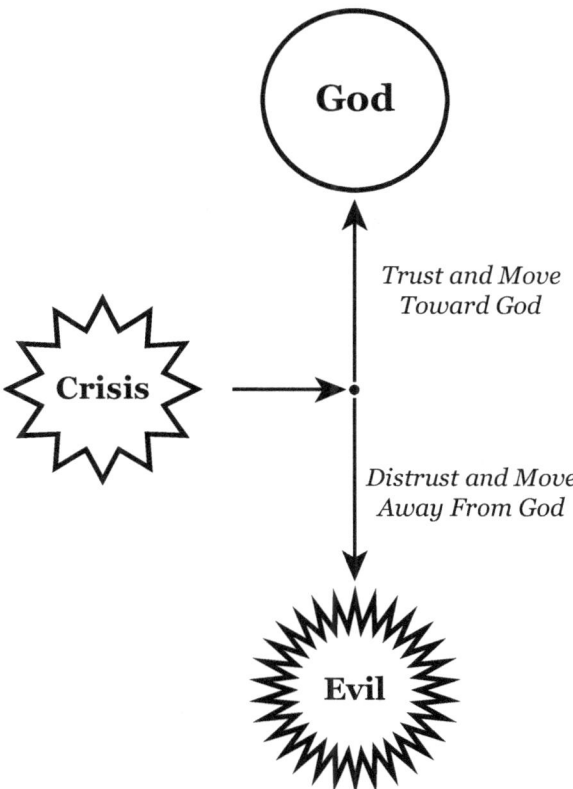

God is always calling you to Himself. Here are three possible resolutions that will move you toward God:
1. *I need to grow and expand the sense of who I am* (develop a more accurate self-image or "you-view").
2. *I need to clarify and correct my understanding of who God is* (develop a more accurate God-image or "God-view").
3. *I need to recognize life isn't what I think it is* (develop a more accurate worldview).

All three resolutions focus in different directions, but growth in any one is ultimately an internal change in perspective and understanding.

During a crisis, your worldview is put to the test. Let your hunger drive you into God's arms (Proverbs 16:26). If you adjust your worldview to be closer to God's reality, you'll learn more about who you are, such as
- where you came from and where you're going,
- what is your responsibility and what is God's, and
- why you trust or don't trust God.

How Will You Respond?

When faced with an identity crisis, you can decide to focus on what you can't control or on what you can control. What you choose will have a great impact on the quality and direction of your life.

How much is within your control? Surprisingly little yet surprisingly much. As you learned in Chapter 3, God creates and sustains an unchangeable reality. But He leaves a lot in your control. You have the freedom to choose good or evil.

How you respond depends on how you perceive God. You'll move toward God or away from God depending on your view of who He is. Becoming aware of why you trust or don't trust God will help you resolve your crisis.

No one asked you if you wanted to be born. God decided to bring you into this world. How do you experience your life? Are you a prisoner or an honored guest? The game Monopoly has a jail space. When you move to the space, you're either locked up or just visiting. In life, are you in jail or just visiting?

God didn't ask you if you wanted to be created, but here you are. And in your crisis, you choose one of three primary attitudes toward God:

1. **Allied:** Your primary response is that of an honored guest. You align yourself with God's reality and accept His control. You're thankful and appreciative; you delight in God and His creation. This means worshiping your Creator first and then enjoying creation as best you can. You balance your effort between doing your part and accepting God's responsibility and design for life. You desire intimacy above all else. You want to know the truth about yourself and God, even when it's hard to hear. Your

predominate attitude will be to trust God—joined with God, you receive healing, surrender to God, accept pain and suffering, openly express pain, and accept reality.

2. **Against:** Your primary response is that of a prisoner captured against his will. A prisoner's primary objective is to acquire enough power and control to escape. Anger toward God can cause anyone to make the attempt to escape, but who can escape God (Psalm 139:7–10)? The rebellious prisoner sees God as the enemy and moves against Him and His creation. In extreme cases, he embraces evil. Freedom from God isn't true freedom. Instead, it is choosing isolation from all that is good. Your predominate attitude will be to hate God—in anger, you blame God, lash out, harbor bitterness, and resist reality.

3. **Avoiding:** Your primary response is that of an unwanted guest. An unwanted guest, feeling shame, will try to stay out of sight. Because you feel God's rejection—even though this is a misconception—you ignore God to ease your pain. Why upset God with your presence if it brings disgust and not delight? Remaining disconnected from God, you're susceptible to worshiping creation instead of the Creator. If you can't know how satisfied God is with you, then enjoying the pleasures of creation is second best. Your predominate attitude will be to ignore God—avoiding pain, you become numb and flee reality.

As you can see, the nature of your response is determined by how much you trust God. Which option best describes your heart condition and life motivation?

Even if you're entrenched in one attitude, each new crisis gives you a fresh opportunity to reevaluate your choice. When bad things happen, or when nothing inspirational occurs, you might question God's existence and goodness. A near escape may instill a feeling that you're particularly blessed. Eventually you'll settle into one of the three responses, usually with more vigor.

So how will you respond to your crisis? Will you move toward God, allow Him to give you what you need, and embrace Him as a friend? Or will you move away from God and reject Him as an enemy? Everyone, has some sort of relationship with God. Where are you on this spectrum?

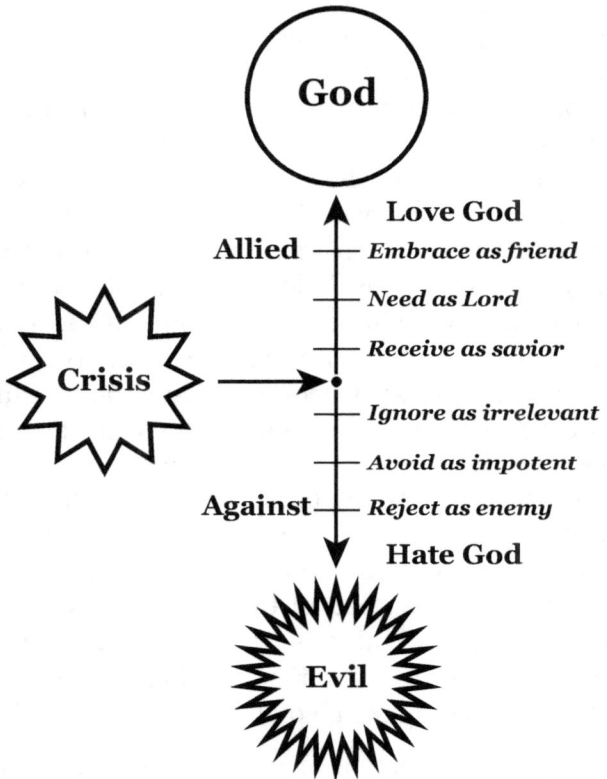

During crises, we have the greatest opportunity to make contact with God and learn how much He cares. Don't give up. The smallest hope that God cares can start you moving toward Him. The momentum of pushing through a crisis is uplifting and faith building.

No one can make sense of life on her own. God designed us, so we only gain meaning from Him. He places the desire for Himself in our hearts. We'll talk more about desires in the next chapter. God is our best and truest ally in any crisis.

Chapter 4 — From Crisis to Crown

Study Questions

1. What is the biggest crisis you're currently facing?
2. Explain how an identity crisis is a spiritual problem.
3. Does your crisis render your view of yourself, God, or the world as obsolete? How?
4. Do you feel more like a prisoner or an honored guest?
5. How much do you trust God when life is difficult or painful?
6. Do you think you're generally aware of evil, or in denial of evil?
7. What is your attitude toward God? Are you allied with, against, or avoiding God?

---

[6] When you became born again, God made you a new creation—spiritually perfect. Yet your flesh remains compromised—diseased and capable of sin—and though considered as good as dead, it must eventually die.

Chapter 5

From Desire to Destiny

We all aspire to fulfill a dream. Some people desire to succeed in business. Others choose full-time ministry. Some people only focus on raising a family. Others desire to join the military. And then there are in-the-moment desires, things we want right away: some rest, perhaps, or encouragement from a friend, or a better job. When you have desires, you also have choices as to how you will fulfill your desires. Let's look at how Mary and Martha, sisters who spent time with Jesus, managed their desires.

As they continued their travel, Jesus entered a village. A woman by the name of Martha welcomed him and made him feel quite at home. She had a sister, Mary, who sat before the Master, hanging on every word he said. But Martha was pulled away by all she had to do in the kitchen. Later, she stepped in, interrupting them. "Master, don't you care that my sister has abandoned the kitchen to me? Tell her to lend me a hand."
The Master said, "Martha, dear Martha, you're fussing far too much and getting yourself worked up over nothing. One thing only is essential, and Mary has chosen it—it's the main course, and won't be taken from her."
—John 10:38–42 (The Message)

Mary chose what she needed emotionally at the time and experienced contentment. Martha chose to serve others and she became irritated. What was Martha's mistake? We know from another passage (John 11:21–27) that Martha had a strong faith. But in this instance, her desire to serve others appears to have overridden her emotional needs. Jesus allowed Martha her choice but prevented her from stealing away Mary's choice. All of us must choose what to do with the time God gives us.

In the movie *The Fellowship of the Ring*, Frodo volunteers to destroy the evil ring. If someone didn't destroy the ring, it would end up destroying all he knew to be good, including his home, the Shire. Frodo didn't understand why such evil would emerge in his lifetime. Gandalf, Frodo's trusted adviser, encouraged him by pointing out that none of us can choose our time in history. Indeed, God chooses many things for us, such as our identity, our family, our birthday, and our time of death. But God gives us the power to choose what to do with our time.

So what do *you* want from life? Your dreams are a major clue. What you want is intimately tied to God's intentions as creator. The good things you want, you want because God gave you the desires. And if God gives you a desire, He also plans to fulfill it.

To be able to strongly desire is a life blessing.

Contrast healthy desire with apathy or no desire. A healthy desire not met is better than an inability to desire at all. But if you haven't had your desire met, don't be concerned. God loves to give gifts to His children—and He gives lavishly (Matthew 7:7–11). God wants to fulfill your desire. Don't stop desiring what is good.

Know Your Desires

When most people think of their desires, they focus on their immediate physical wants. But God also created you with emotional and kingdom desires, which provide a deeper level of satisfaction—joy that can't be found elsewhere.

If we find ourselves with a desire that nothing in this world can satisfy, the most probable explanation is that we were made for another world.
—C.S. Lewis

Chapter 5 — From Desire to Destiny

Think of the physical, emotional, and kingdom desires as three stomachs, each with its distinct appetite or craving. There's plenty of hunger to go around, yet overeating is futile. Overfilling one stomach can't compensate for starving another. You can be distracted by your easier-to-fill desires with all their intense cravings. Physical desires tend to be more easily satisfied than emotional desires, but the satisfaction won't last as long. And kingdom desires provide a whole other level of satisfaction that can't be met by the other desires.

Let's examine these different types of desires more closely.

Physical Desires

Physical desires consist of all the cravings we have as we seek to meet our physical needs. Basic physical desires are hunger for food and drink. Others objects of desire include sleep, exercise, entertainment, physical affection, and sexual gratification.

Some physical desires are needs and some are wants. What you need for survival and what you want for comfort should remain as separate categories.

Be flexible with your wants, willing to sacrifice them, but be assertive with your needs. The majority of things in life are optional—you don't need them in order to fulfill your life's purpose. For example, have you ever spent a whole weekend binge-watching a TV show? Some desires are merely distractions and not essential for fulfillment. Instant pleasure from physical fulfillment is different than lasting joy from spiritual fulfillment.

Emotional Desires

Emotional desires speak to who you are as a relational being. They drive you to attach to others so you can experience the truth about your identity.

Meeting these desires is as important as meeting your physical desires for food and shelter. God created you to be in relationship with others. Through knowing and being known, you can feast on acceptance, encouragement, truth, and mercy. Don't sacrifice your emotional needs for your physical wants. Internal contentment is better than external satisfaction.

Relationships are God's delivery system for all emotional needs.[7] God intentionally puts people into your life who care about you and can provide emotional support. But there is a risk involved: people can let you down. Expecting any particular person to meet all of your needs is a recipe for frustration and even disaster.

God is ultimately the one responsible for meeting your emotional needs. No other person is completely capable like God. He is a friend that sticks closer than a brother (see Proverbs 18:24). He is the great Comforter and Father of mercies (see 2 Corinthians 1:3–5).

Here are five longings God meets when you submit to Him as His child:

1. **Unconditional Love and Acceptance:** God knows who you really are. He sees you at your best and your worst. He's never going to give up on you, not even when you're at your worst. God is love.
2. **Persisting Hope:** God has a plan to make life better. At some point in the future, life is guaranteed to be made perfect, and it will last forever. Until then, you can accept that God wants you to endure life's difficulties and grow in faithfulness.
3. **Imminent Purpose:** God has a specific purpose for your existence. He created you unique, so your active participation is essential. God matched your identity to your destiny—the work He envisioned for you (Ephesians 2:10). You aren't optional or replaceable; You're significant and important. You're not an accident; God made you, exactly as you are, on purpose.
4. **Meaningful Connection:** God participates in an interactive relationship with you. God wants a dialogue with you. God cares about your feelings. He is your permanent, loving parent.
5. **Faithful Security:** God is always with you. He will never abandon you. He will never leave you or forsake you (Deuteronomy 31:6). No matter what happens in this life, God is on your side.

Fear not, for I am with you;
be not dismayed, for I am your God;

Chapter 5 — From Desire to Destiny

*I will strengthen you, I will help you,
I will uphold you with my righteous right hand.*
—Isaiah 41:10

You won't be able to comprehend much of life unless your emotional desires are being met. If you're unsatisfied with some aspect of life, this probably means a basic emotional need is being neglected. When these needs go unmet, let this frustration drive you back to God.

To move toward God, express your honest feelings—your deepest desires—in order to receive His comfort. Open your heart to God by crying out with your longings. God wants to provide comfort, but don't expect to be pain-free in this life. When your emotional needs are met, you'll experience peace and contentment even in the face of aggravating circumstances. You'll have what is better—what no one else can steal from you.

Kingdom Desires

God's kingdom is primarily spiritual. Christians worship God in spirit and truth (John 4:24). Serving God is a practical application of worship. Your soul's most basic spiritual desire is to find purpose. That longing for purpose is satisfied as you advance God's kingdom. Spiritual desires are tied into your emotional desires. Usually, when your spiritual self is being satisfied, so are your emotional needs. Because spiritual fulfillment requires sacrifice, you must be mature enough to willingly accept the cost of your spiritual pursuits.

Just as everyone has physical and emotional desires, everyone has spiritual desires too. We all worship something. Those who seek God will find Him. Those who want a different god will find another way to try to meet their spiritual needs. But this is a corruption of spiritual desire. Binging on junk food will end in obesity; using people for emotional fulfillment will end in heartbreak; and seeking a god of your own making will end in spiritual bankruptcy.

When you seek God to meet your spiritual desires, you'll also want to pursue Christlikeness. When Paul explains contentment to Timothy, he mentions several examples of Christlike behavior: righteousness, godliness, faith, love, endurance, and gentleness.

> *But godliness with contentment is great gain. For we brought nothing into the world, and we can take nothing out of it. But if we have food and clothing, we will be content with that. Those who want to get rich fall into temptation and a trap and into many foolish and harmful desires that plunge people into ruin and destruction. For the love of money is a root of all kinds of evil. Some people, eager for money, have wandered from the faith and pierced themselves with many griefs. But you, man of God, flee from all this, and pursue righteousness, godliness, faith, love, endurance and gentleness.*
> —1 Timothy 6:6–11

Rescue Your Desires

Have you made the things of life more important than God intended? Are you eager for money? Maybe you ached too hard for the wrong things and ended up getting what you wanted. If you don't exercise self-control, all the things you collected may hinder you from fulfilling God's purpose for your life.

In the movie *The Matrix,* a main character named Cypher betrays his friends by requesting to be returned to the false but comfortable reality he once enjoyed. He exchanges his relationships for physical pleasure.

What if you've become numb to emotional and kingdom desires, and you can't enjoy the physical ones like you used to? Perhaps you've become addicted to physical desires (sex, food, possessions, or exercise) precisely because you didn't know how to satisfy your emotional and kingdom desires. Or you might be addicted to emotional desires instead, trying to meet your longings through unhealthy relationships.

It's easy to get distracted by physical and emotional needs and neglect your spiritual life. As long as your self-image remains significantly distorted, you won't be able to experience what God

Chapter 5 — From Desire to Destiny

has planned for you. But there is hope even if you've given into your desires and they're all mixed up.

Jesus had other food that satisfied His soul (John 4:31–38). God didn't create within you the capacity to achieve fulfillment through satisfying your physical or emotional desires alone. Complete fulfillment requires you to satisfy all of your God-given physical, emotional, and kingdom desires.

If you get off track and are feeding one desire more than another, it's time to refocus. If you're eating more food than your body needs to soothe emotional or spiritual distress, become still and take inventory of your life. Trying to meet emotional or spiritual needs with food is like attempting to quench your thirst with salt water or nourish your body with candy. It's a false hope. Your cravings will never be fulfilled. It's time to rescue your desires.

Hunger and satisfaction must be equal partners in order for you to grow spiritually. You need to be able to tolerate feeling unfulfilled to appreciate fulfillment. Balancing these feelings brings stability, strength, and security. Imbalanced desire creates fear, insecurity, and desperation.

A jealous person doesn't become secure by acquiring what others have. His jealousy is driven by his emotional longings, not by what he actually has in a given moment. He can only become secure by focusing on what he needs and choosing not to fixate on what others have.

Ecclesiastes suggests you accept what life provides as you make the most of what God has given to you (Ecclesiastes 5:8–20; 6:7). You can develop the ability to accept and adapt to circumstances beyond your control.

> **Aching for what you know God wants to provide is the path to righteous living.**

You can be starving for lack of a healthy desire. When you ache for the right stuff, you'll be completely fulfilled. It's possible to be hungry and fulfilled at the same time.

Blessed are the poor in spirit,
for theirs is the kingdom of heaven.

TO IDENTITY AND BEYOND

Blessed are those who hunger and thirst for righteousness, for they will be filled.
—Matthew 5:3, 6

Whether you have a lot and feel full, or you have little and feel empty, you can always hunger for more that only God can provide. In any circumstance, trust and depend upon God for spiritual and earthly needs. Acknowledge and validate your healthy needs. Trust God to meet them.

You can stop seeking perfect satisfaction and still find fulfillment. You don't require a perfect life in order to feel content. Once you understand this, you can accept what you have with thankfulness. When Job lost everything, he was understandably devastated, but he didn't give up his integrity; he didn't give up his faith in God.

Then his wife said to him, "Do you still hold fast your integrity? Curse God and die." But he said to her, "You speak as one of the foolish women would speak. Shall we receive good from God, and shall we not receive evil?" In all this Job did not sin with his lips.
—Job 2:9–10

No matter how bad life gets or how poor you become, God promises to never give up on you. Enough money for "daily bread" is good. Enough money for kingdom purposes is good. But money stored up for personal security as a substitute for God is idolatry.

Keep your life free from love of money, and be content with what you have, for he has said, "I will never leave you nor forsake you." So we can confidently say, "The Lord is my helper; I will not fear; what can man do to me?"
—Hebrews 13:5–6

Chapter 5 — From Desire to Destiny

Prioritize Your Desires

To live confidently in the Lord, you should periodically rebalance your priorities. First make sure you understand all your needs, and then consider the best way to prioritize them. Are you putting your physical needs over your emotional and spiritual needs? Are you focusing on your spiritual needs at the neglect of your emotional needs?

When you prioritize your desires in a balanced fashion, you invite freedom and efficiency in your life. If you don't effectively prioritize your desires, you'll end up filling up on superficial desires first. You might not even be aware you have other desires.

Think of yourself as a box in which all your desires have to fit. In the figure on the left, you see how the physical desires are getting priority and forcing out the emotional and kingdom desires. In the figure on the right, you see a healthy balance where all the desires are being met.

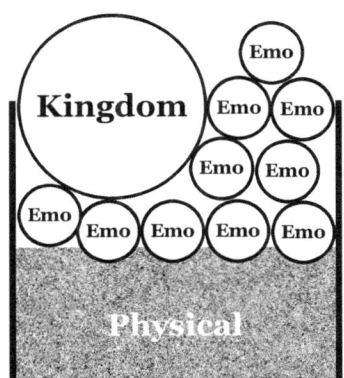
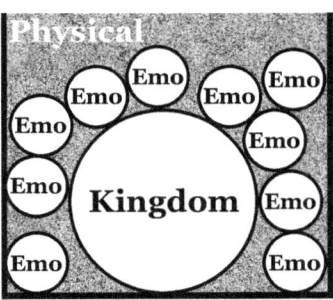

As you start your day, you might do a quick examination. Will you be doing anything today that counts toward kingdom purposes and fulfills emotional desires? Are you establishing healthy ways to meet your physical desires?

> **You'll experience abundant living when you prioritize according to what God considers most important.**

Correctly prioritized, all your reasonable desires can be met in your life. You might still give up some physical desires to fit in the more important desires, but the tradeoff will enrich your life in many ways (Matthew 6:32). For example, you can stop drinking alcohol to calm your nerves, and start spending quality time with your family. You can skip some selfish, mindless entertainment, and talk to God about how you're doing. You can give God the best part of your day so He can help you prioritize.

All of your desires are good, provided you fulfill them in the right way. If your physical stomach is full, overfilling it won't satisfy your emotional or spiritual appetites.

Don't replace your desire for God with a desire for anything else. You can enjoy life as much as possible; just don't focus on pleasure at the expense of building God's kingdom.

You can have what you want if you can prove you don't need it.

If you desire not to be alone or lonely, that is also God's desire. Getting married may or may not be the solution. How can you align your appetite to God's reality without losing yourself in the process? You might think God wants you to be miserable. No, just the opposite. However, you need to correct your priorities for everything to fall into place. Make sure your priorities align with God's priorities, which are to love Him, love others, and tell people about His love.

If you want to be (or remain) married, work to strengthen your identity to such a place where your happiness doesn't depend on being married. Instead of looking to someone else to complete your identity, focus on how you can be a blessing for another person—and then enter marriage with that attitude. This advice would save many from divorce.

When you desire something in a desperately dysfunctional way, you'll likely act impulsively and make a poor decision. You'll use creation the wrong way instead of acting with righteousness, or right-use-ness. What is God's intended purpose for the object of your desire? If you can reprioritize your desires, you can reverse the effects of an addiction.

Chapter 5 — From Desire to Destiny

The best way to develop healthy desires is with support from others as you seek God through fasting, His Word, and prayer. Healthy fasting resets your habits. In order to create a new routine, you must create space by allowing old habits to fade away from disuse. When you temporarily devalue physical desires, you train yourself to be satisfied in other ways. Denying fulfillment of simple pleasures allows you to better connect with your other desires. Then, you'll experience deeper satisfaction.

If you pursue your emotional and kingdom desires with gusto, physical temptations will wane. You'll find it easier to adjust your appetite and become thankful for the opportunities God provides to enjoy life—intimate friendships, healthy food, moderate exercise, and a mutually satisfying sex life (if you're married). When you consider and then honor God's intentions for His creation, you'll cherish the people around you and enjoy the resources God provides.

To reach contentment, you must be comfortable whether you have a lot or have little.

What are the minimum thresholds of shelter, sustenance, and relational support required for your satisfaction? Your answers will help you regain the balance you need between all your desires. You'll be surprised by how little you actually need. Allow yourself to feel your desires, anticipating the greater spiritual fulfillment that God has for you.

To reach contentment, you must develop the hunger of your kingdom stomach. You must long for what God longs for; otherwise, you'll attempt to overstuff your other stomachs. You might rush into a marriage before you're ready for it, or take on a higher mortgage than you can afford—and your kingdom stomach will remain empty. On the other hand, if you can stay patient and measured in your physical and emotional pursuits, you'll have fewer concerns to distract you from your spiritual desires.

Don't ignore or numb your unfulfilled desires. Instead, like Paul, control your desires so you can be content in both poverty and riches, hunger and fullness. When you're connected to God and fulfilled by pursuing His purposes, you have the strength and faith to trust that God will meet your needs.

> *Not that I am speaking of being in need, for I have learned in whatever situation I am to be content. I know how to be brought low, and I know how to abound. In any and every circumstance, I have learned the secret of facing plenty and hunger, abundance and need. I can do all things through him who strengthens me.*
> —Philippians 4:11–13

Putting God first in your life changes how you desire.

When you have the Holy Spirit, you'll never thirst the same way again. This allows you to be satisfied even when life doesn't work in your favor.

> *Jesus answered, "Everyone who drinks this water will be thirsty again, but whoever drinks the water I give them will never thirst. Indeed, the water I give them will become in them a spring of water welling up to eternal life."*
> —John 4:13–14

When you put God first, He will gently transform your desires into healthy desires that surge with life. God doesn't rip away your heart's desire and replace it something you never really wanted. He doesn't give you some kind of spiritual lobotomy. You won't be left resenting God for changing your desires. You can trust your desires, provided they are prioritized and pure. Love God and do what you want.

You'll never go unfulfilled when you're living out exactly who God made you to be.

Chapter 5 — From Desire to Destiny

That statement should encourage you to reflect on your alignment with God's reality. If you like the same kind of things as God, you'll be fulfilled. If you're not fulfilled, then you're probably not understanding and living out exactly who God made you to be.

---

*Take delight in the Lord,
and he will give you the desires of your heart.*
—Psalm 37:4

God wants you to experience life to its fullest (John 10:10). You can live an abundant life by seeing life through God's eyes. God's will for your life includes the fulfillment of the desires He has given to you. Everything is "Yes in Christ." But the road to fulfillment has potholes, as we'll explore in the next section.

Endure Your Desires

Endure means to suffer through. Once you've tasted what it's like to pursue God's kingdom, you'll probably pass on some temporal desires. Sometimes you'll surrender an honest desire by choice; other times people or opportunities will withdraw from your reach. It's essential to fully grieve these losses. When you lose something important and irreplaceable, you suffer. The Apollo 13 crew lost the opportunity to visit the moon. Samwise lost his best friend Frodo. Jesus lost His intimate connection to the Father, enduring His wrath, if only for a moment (see Hebrews 12).

I grieve my unmet desires by telling God, *When all this is over, when we're all safe in heaven for eternity, I'd like to spend a few hundred years just resting, just playing games, just going on a long hike, just for fun. No worries. No disappointments. No more suffering.*

You're a temporary citizen of the world; your real citizenship is in heaven. Don't get too comfortable with this life. Keep one foot in eternity (heaven) and one foot in your present circumstances. Don't be so heavenly minded you're no earthly good. Likewise, don't be so earthly minded that you're no heavenly good. Maintain a balance between action and contentment; don't be complacent, yet accept the life God provides.

If you can pass on worldly fulfillment, you'll be disentangled from the cares of the world and alive with purpose. You'll be free to be a world-changer—to contribute and not just consume. You're experiencing true freedom when you no longer feel compelled to overfill your desires—when you understand that "to live is Christ and to die is gain" (Philippians 1:21).

Fill up enough so you have a life worth living—then sacrifice for God's greater purposes, because the world as we know it is passing away.

What I mean, brothers and sisters, is that the time is short. From now on those who have wives should live as if they do not; those who mourn, as if they did not; those who are happy, as if they were not; those who buy something, as if it were not theirs to keep; those who use the things of the world, as if not engrossed in them. For this world in its present form is passing away.
—1 Corinthians 7:29–31

Material possessions are disposable; you can't take them with you into heaven. Consider this when choosing where to invest your greatest effort (Matthew 6:21). There is a time to seek to have your needs met in order to build trust with God, and there is a time to deny self and push God's agenda forward. After you've prioritized your desires, all that remains to do is to accept suffering when it comes into your life. Sometimes God calls you to a longer period of hunger than you'd like.

You can reach a place where being satisfied by the things of this life isn't necessary. Accept life for what it is. Life can be messy and tragic. You might be sold on the false idea that you have to have more possessions in order to experience peace and contentment. Consider daily meditation to practice calming your brain and your body; in this way you can experience a physical contentment.

Chapter 5 — From Desire to Destiny

When you know for sure, by faith, that a better reality is coming, you can experience a fullness that no circumstances can take away. Anticipating a better reality to come is its own reward (Romans 8:18). Then you're free to make a difference in the time you have, just as Jesus did.

The desire to be accepted and loved is strong. If you're unable to tolerate the negatives in life, or if you haven't experienced enough positives, you might choose to close your heart to God and drift away from Him. But no matter where you are with God, if you open your heart to seeking Him, you can move back toward Him. The choice to move away from or toward God is the focus of the next two chapters.

Study Questions

1. What is the deepest fulfillment you can imagine?
2. In what ways are your dreams fulfilled or unfulfilled?
3. Often we hesitate to lament our deepest sorrows. Do you have a secret grief in your heart? Why haven't you shared your pain?
4. What do you long for in this life that God also longs for?
5. How well can you tolerate desire without immediate fulfillment?
6. What can you do now to minimize any significant regrets for how you lived?
7. Can you identify a desire that is blocking your pursuit of God's kingdom?
8. Read Hebrews 12. What can be shaken from your life? What is impossible to shake from your life?
9. Make a list of your values and desires. Sort them from most important to least important. Now make a second list according to how you actually live. Compare the lists to see how you might bring your actual life into alignment with your ideal life. If helpful, categorize them into physical, emotional, or kingdom desires.

---

[7] First heard from Christian authors Henry Cloud and John Townsend.

Chapter 6

Overcome Opposition

Some people experience unbelievable suffering. They've been abused, and they know it. Others recall no abuse and assume they had a great childhood.

When Samantha looks back on her childhood, she feels guilty. *I have no reason to feel so sad. I should be thankful I wasn't abused.*

Neglect is trickier to identify than abuse—it passes as normal. If you asked Samantha, that's what she'd say. *I had a normal, good childhood.* When her parents divorced when she was thirteen, her dad promised to spend time with her every week—a promise he broke. He didn't yell at her, but he didn't call her either. In fact, he never showed up for their scheduled time. Since nothing happened, it should be easy for Samantha to move on, right? But Samantha didn't have the opportunity to say, *Dad, I'm disappointed you didn't keep your promise.*

Samantha's self-image suffered, and so did her view of God. Abuse is receiving what you didn't need, while neglect is not receiving what you needed. Both steal the security and certainty many take for granted.

The word *disappoint* comes from the French *disappointer,* which means to remove from office.[8] Samantha is a Christian, so in her disappointment she *dethroned* God in her heart. She felt God had betrayed her, and she became bitter toward Him. Nothing pleases Satan more than when a resentful Christian distrusts God.

Maybe you didn't receive what you needed. Perhaps you've been repeatedly disappointed and felt like telling God, *You're fired!*

Guarding your heart while you're in the middle of an encounter with evil is necessary. Sometimes it continues to feel necessary after the threat is gone. Trusting God isn't easy when He has allowed evil to touch your life. But if you want to restore your emotional health, you must become vulnerable again so you can reorient yourself to God's reality.

Evil forces are waiting to pounce on us when we're weak and weary, and then distract us from knowing our true identities and the goodness of God's reality. You have an enemy who seeks to cripple you. Your enemy is spiritual, not any physical person. When people sin against you, they align themselves with evil, but they aren't the true enemy.

Be sober-minded; be watchful. Your adversary the devil prowls around like a roaring lion, seeking someone to devour.
For we do not wrestle against flesh and blood, but against the rulers, against the authorities, against the cosmic powers over this present darkness, against the spiritual forces of evil in the heavenly places.
—1 Peter 5:8; Ephesians 6:12

Samantha's dad isn't her enemy. But he wounded her, and this has made her heart vulnerable to the lies of her true enemy. She needs to be careful she doesn't slip and find herself cornered by a hungry lion.

Sustained, elevated pain needs time to heal. If you're broken, stuck, wounded, hurting, or lost, then seek help from those whom God provides. Go for deeper healing and intensive help. God's not the problem. God is sad when you're suffering. In your pain, you may doubt God's power or intentions, but God will never reject you or regret who He made you to be. God doesn't want you to feel ashamed.

But on a bad day, even at 24 years old, Samantha thinks, *If God is good, why do I suffer and despise my life? Why, like Job, do I wish I was never born?*

Samantha attempted a compromise. She would hold onto her belief in God while also remaining angry at Him. This put her on a slippery slope moving away from God because hating God starts with distrust.

If you harden your heart to God, you may feel safe for the moment. But as long as you remain deceived and in the dark about

Chapter 6 — Overcome Opposition

God, you won't trust Him enough to let Him heal your past injuries. The answer can't be to push God away, but when faced with a big enough offense, it can seem like the only tolerable option.

This chapter is for those who feel betrayed by God and can't bring themselves to let their guard down and trust God again. While this may be difficult to read, I'm including it to encourage you: At any point in your journey, no matter how far away you find yourself from God, you can seek God and return to Him.

The Slippery Slope to Hating God

Hating God starts with the seemingly innocent *I don't need God's help.*

A joke I heard some time ago highlights prideful independence. A man driving through a parking lot on a busy shopping day is having difficulty finding a parking spot. He stops to say a quick prayer: "God, please help me find a place to park my car so I can finish shopping." As he finishes his prayer, he looks up and sees an open spot. "Oh, never mind, God. I've got this."

Turning away from God is a progressive disease. Once you start down that path, you can quickly proceed from a bitter heart to a heart that hates God. The dangerous path leads to progressively darker places. We're going to explore in detail three levels of hating and distrusting God.

Level of Hating God	Level of Distrusting God
1: Ignore God as irrelevant	Subconscious Distrust
2: Avoid God as impotent	Active Distrust
3: Reject God as enemy	Aggressive Distrust

How you relate to God depends on what you've already experienced in life. If you don't receive enough affirmation of who you are in life, you won't be able to see God as good. On the other hand, if you receive too much wealth and favor without connecting that all good things are from God, you'll decide that you don't need God. Either way, you would lack enough practical experience and contact with God to allow you to trust Him. Prosperity and hardship can each drive a person to desire independence from God.

God wired you to desire perfection, so wanting life to go smoothly isn't wrong. However, you have no choice but to live in God's broken reality: a cursed and dying world. Fortunately, God also wired you to accept good enough. To have a chance to connect with God, there has to be a middle ground—your life experiences need to fall within the window of optimal comfort.

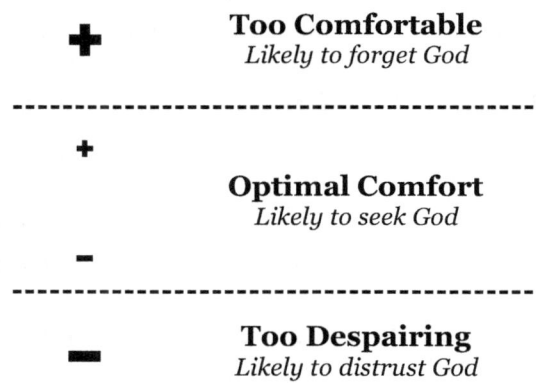

God doesn't want you to needlessly suffer. But your main purpose in life can't be to avoid all suffering. First, it will never happen. Second, knowing God amidst suffering is better than not knowing God and being comfortable. Satan's strategies to thwart your alliance with God involve complacency and suffering. If he can't get you to despair because of suffering or guilt, he'll get you so comfortable that you won't feel your need for God.

---

*Two things I ask of you;
deny them not to me before I die:
Remove far from me falsehood and lying;
give me neither poverty nor riches;
feed me with the food that is needful for me,
lest I be full and deny you
and say, "Who is the LORD?"
or lest I be poor and steal
and profane the name of my God.*
—Proverbs 30:7–9

Level 1: Ignore God as Irrelevant

You ignore God when you don't feel you need Him. You have no interest in searching out the meaning of life because you're preoccupied with your day-to-day life. You're complacent—happy with superficial satisfaction. Your life is on autopilot. You've stopped paddling your boat, and the current is taking you slowly downstream away from God. You take on an attitude of indifference toward God. Unfortunately, if you ignore God, you'll inevitably drift away from Him. You're not seeking after evil, but when you witness others' suffering, you're not motivated to become personally involved. You don't want to awaken a sleeping giant; deep down you're discontented.

Let's look at three characteristics of people who ignore God: distracted, naïve, and selfish.

Characteristic #1: Distracted

Having too much and being able to fill your life with whatever you want can be detrimental to your relationship with God.

You could be so successful (life is much more than you expected) that you're satiated and enamored with what this life offers, and therefore God's goodness seems irrelevant. If you experience too much goodness (without connecting it to God), you'll conclude that you have no need for God, thinking some other providence is supplying what you need.

This bypasses the desire to seek a deeper understanding of God and self, placing life's comforts and pleasures above God's calling and purpose. Your treasures will be found on earth, and you won't expend any effort to explore the deeper reality.

Falling in love with something other than God is easy. Because of unhealthy desires, your heart can become lost in many diverse experiences. You need to grow up experiencing enough good, but not so much that you're spoiled. Otherwise, you'll be too distracted, and you'll never want to (or be able to) know yourself or God.

The young man said to him, "All these I have kept. What do I still lack?" Jesus said to him, "If you would be perfect, go, sell what you possess

> *and give to the poor, and you will have treasure in heaven; and come, follow me." When the young man heard this he went away sorrowful, for he had great possessions.*
> —Matthew 19:20–22

People can also ignore God when they don't know what is happening around them. Because of a lack of identity, they let their environment or culture define who they are. Consider how the Romans kept the masses pacified by providing cheap food and entertainment (Bread and Circus). They distracted the people and created a false sense of peace. The same distractions are available to us today.

If you don't understand how life really works, you may simply drift along and indulge in day-to-day living. Pleasure and comfort become the main prize. You shut down and spend time overwhelming your senses so you don't have to encounter who you are (or the self-image that you feel ashamed of).

In C.S. Lewis's book *The Screwtape Letters*, the demon Wormwood's uncle says, "I had not forgotten my promise to consider whether we should make the patient an extreme patriot or an extreme pacifist. All extremes, except extreme devotion to the Enemy, are to be encouraged.... Some ages are lukewarm and complacent, and then it is our business to soothe them yet faster asleep. Other ages, of which the present is one, are unbalanced and prone to faction, and it is our business to inflame them...that [they] may acquire the uneasy intensity and the defensive self-righteousness...."[9]

If you blindly trust worldly authorities, you too can easily be deceived or pacified by Satan, the government, or worldly culture. You can become lulled into a false sense of peace and contentment through relative prosperity and creature comforts. You can be brainwashed by the surrounding culture into chasing after the worldly status quo.

Characteristic #2: Naïve

People can drift away from God because of a lack of experience with evil. You may be ignorant of evil and think your freedom is secure. You think, *I'm safe. Tragedy won't come to my doorstep in my lifetime.* And since it hasn't yet, you haven't been forced to develop a more sophisticated worldview and healthier self-image.

Naiveté can result from an innocent state of ignorance. Recall from Chapter 4 how Pippin wanted to run away from the brewing war and return to his blissful life in the Shire. Merry reminded Pippin that "there won't be a Shire" if they didn't do something. If you're naïve, you follow along with what everyone else is doing without questioning why or looking to see if there is a better way.

Another way to be naïve is through prideful ignorance. You may be in awe of the world's advancements in technology and general knowledge. You've become so enamored with human progress that you decide you can't believe spiritual forces are real. You think, *We can overcome life's difficulties without God's help.*

And so you don't even bother to consider the existence of God—someone who is responsible and can help. If God is out of sight, He is out of mind. Some people put their hope in technology, anticipating the day when humans might extend their life indefinitely with new biological or robotic body parts.

Denial of evil is a third way to be naïve. To protect your sense of well-being, you deny the realities of evil. *Ignorance is bliss* sums it up all too well. Even when others are suffering, the default response is to look the other way. As long as you're safe, you'll accept the benefits without the fight. You'll ignore the stakes.

Characteristic #3: Selfish

People can drift away from God by standing by and letting others fight for freedom and the niceties of life that they enjoy. If you're satisfied enough with life, you won't put the effort in to take a stand. You'll do the least required, and let someone else do the hard work.

Selfishness is selling out others to save your own skin: betraying others, choosing pleasure, denying that the pleasure won't last, ignoring evil. These actions never turn out well for anyone, but they seem good and safe at the time.

Judas is an extreme example of someone caught up with the spirit of evil. The Bible calls him a thief and proclaims that Satan entered him. He agreed to betray Jesus for only thirty pieces of silver. He regularly preached fiscal responsibility while stealing from the poor. He was deceived into thinking the money was worth the cost of betrayal.

> *Then Satan entered Judas, called Iscariot, one of the Twelve. And Judas went to the chief priests and the officers of the temple guard and discussed with them how he might betray Jesus.*
> —Luke 22:3–4 (NIV)

Judas progressed all the way down the slippery slope until at last he was deceived into hating God. But this started with greed, a relatively minor sin compared to being complicit in murdering Jesus. In the end, he recognized the evil but wasn't able to fully remove himself from it. Instead, he died in the despair and insanity of someone who betrayed God.

> *Then when Judas, his betrayer, saw that Jesus was condemned, he changed his mind and brought back the thirty pieces of silver to the chief priests and the elders, saying, "I have sinned by betraying innocent blood." They said, "What is that to us? See to it yourself." And throwing down the pieces of silver into the temple, he departed, and he went and hanged himself.*
> —Matthew 27:3–5

Lando Calrissian, a Star Wars character from the movie *The Empire Strikes Back*, fell for the same scheme. He sold out his friend, Han Solo, to make a deal with their enemy, Darth Vader. He thought he had a good deal at first, but when Darth Vader had what he wanted, he continued to change the deal until Lando had virtually nothing. Fortunately for Han, Lando eventually atoned for his betrayal.

If you find yourself at Level 1, then moving back toward God involves confessing how you've been too focused on your own comfort at the expense of others and your own spiritual life. If you don't get off the slope, you might end up falling to Level 2.

Level 2: Avoid God as Impotent

Many people try to make life work without God because of personal pain. Samantha experienced pain firsthand. She didn't know what to do with God because He seemed powerless to protect her.

By the time you decide to escape God, you've developed real reasons for doing so. You're no longer just witnessing evil visit your neighbor's house—it's come knocking on your door. You openly admit your distrust of God, believing God is less than perfect.

God places numerous constraints on us. Even though this is out of love and not sinister in any way, we don't often appreciate being told what not to do. People within Level 2 are convinced God has short-changed them, and so they determine to live outside of God's boundaries.

The main difference between ignoring God and avoiding Him is awareness and intentionality. When you're ignoring, you might have a nagging feeling in the back of your mind that God can't be trusted. But to avoid God, you must commit yourself to life without God and develop skills to cope without God.

When you haven't had enough good experiences in life to realize that something better is possible, you may simply assume God doesn't care about you. But you can't live in ignorance for long when pain from negative experiences piles up. Eventually you must either go to God in desperation or choose to keep your distance.

Let's examine three characteristics of people who avoid God: wounded, bitter, and prideful.

Characteristic #1: Wounded

For life to make sense, you have to experience a sufficient amount of goodness. Without glimpses of God and His goodness, you'll never have a reason to put your faith in Him. When you're wounded by life, you can become jaded and discouraged. Life will feel too random to believe God exists. You can become so disillusioned—life has been so much less than you hoped it would be—that being numb or addicted is preferred over reality.

When you're burned by life, blaming God is easy. When stuck in pain, you avoid God because you associate suffering with Him. You choose numbness rather than enduring pain and fighting for a cause. As mentioned at the beginning of this chapter, abuse and neglect are the primary ways people feel betrayed by God.

The younger and more vulnerable you are, the more you need to be sheltered from evil. When you suffer a trauma before you've had a chance to develop an understanding of the world and your identity, the emotional wound is severe. It may take a long time to heal and regain what you lost, and you'll need to work to recover the belief that God is good.

Samantha felt abandoned, but that didn't match with God's promise, *I'll never leave you.* She felt trapped in a reality she didn't understand. She had experienced too much pain and suffering, but not enough encounters with a positive God. *I'm suffering too much for God to be real.*

The suffering caused her to form a negative view of God. She doubted God cared, seeing Him as uninvolved and unreachable. In her situation, distrusting God made sense because there wasn't enough good happening to counter the amount of bad.[10]

When you're hurt, a typical first response is to throw up your defenses and say, *I'll never allow myself to be in a such a vulnerable spot again.* When you're feeling betrayed by God, you can react to your hurt and humiliation by refusing to submit, love, and obey. Since God's reality doesn't seem to be true, you'll try to replace it with the safest alternative (of your own making) you can find.

Characteristic #2: Bitter

Betrayal creates suffering, which can lead anyone to become bitter toward God and work to avoid Him. Bitterness usually starts off as an attempt to control what happens in life. Bitterness is often expressed as a complaint and a demand: *God, make my life better. Now!* But God doesn't respond to ultimatums.

Samantha neither denied God nor pursued Him. Instead, she relied on creation. She wanted the benefits God claimed to offer without having to risk intimacy with a God who betrayed her. Holding on in this way kept her brokenness just beyond her awareness. Digging for her own treasures allowed her to passively escape her disappointment in God.

This meant avoiding God, the truth, pain, and needed change. Samantha became disconnected from reality. Her heartbreak resulted in low self-esteem. She presented a tough exterior but remained tender and fragile underneath.

Samantha didn't want to face how she really felt about herself. She couldn't see a positive self-image. She struggled with shame and pride and sought happiness above all else.

She stopped worshipping God and gave herself over to creation. Acting on impulse, she used creation to satisfy her relational needs. She developed an addiction to food and sex that allowed her to block out her suffering. She stopped trying to find a real answer to the difficult question, *How can God be good if life is so full of suffering?*

When someone is addicted to something other than God, selfishness and stubbornness will persist until she experiences enough of God's goodness (James 4:4–6).

Do you deny the reality of a good God because of prolonged suffering? Unfortunately, you can't have happiness in this life without also embracing suffering. To the degree you're unwilling to feel your pain, you'll be unable to experience happiness and joy. In a world where both joy and suffering are possible, you must choose between embracing both or becoming numb.

To be healthy, don't limit yourself to one emotion; instead, seek to genuinely express a full spectrum of emotions. The primary emotions are happy, sad, fearful, angry, and ashamed.

Characteristic #3: Prideful

A prideful heart refuses to need God and so stands in opposition to God. People who can't see God's goodness can respond with pride and indignation. They have a strong sense of independence.

Samantha suffered because God allowed evil to touch her life. She declared that God was weak, God was defective, and God had failed. She believed she could do better than God and better without God.

King Saul insincerely approached God. He kept choosing what seemed right in his own eyes instead of what God declared was right. Even though God gave him specific instructions to wait and rely on the prophet Samuel, Saul decided to move forward with his own idea. He was self-focused instead of God-focused, and this condition only grew worse over the course of his life. He drifted away from God and wasn't able to overcome the sin in his heart. Saul foolishly disobeyed God and eventually pleaded to be put out of his misery after a mortal battle wound.

King David struggled with pride in a different way. He was blind to his arrogance and self-centeredness. His serious sins included adultery and murder. However, in contrast to King Saul, he presented a heart of sincere devotion to God. He made many good choices that honored God. Whether on his own or at the prompting of others, he repented and brought his heart back into alignment with God.

Samantha became so angry at God that she decided she would rather live bitter and away from God than close to a God who allowed her to suffer. She desired autonomy because she distrusted God. *He could stop the pain, but He doesn't. I hate God so much that I'd rather be away from God in hell than at God's side in heaven.*

Finding yourself unable to trust God is the worst place to be in life. When you're angry at God, you cut Him out of your life. You attempt to make it through life without Him. You stop allowing yourself to feel your need for God. If you can't trust Him to meet your need, you won't rely on Him. Therefore, you pursue autonomy from God by denying dependence upon God.

This might look like any of the following:

- You conceal your bottomless pit of need because you fear experiencing your own discomfort. Nobody seems eager to help you, and you're ashamed to ask.
- You're not interested in learning about your true self.
- You've set out to provide for yourself and prove you don't need God.
- You believe if you work hard enough, you'll avoid suffering. Your life goal is to make life the nicest place possible. You'd rather work hard than experience your need for God.
- You're neglecting your work because you're addicted to physical fulfillment (Ecclesiastes 7:4).

If you find yourself at Level 2, then moving back toward God involves confessing how you've been allowing your bitterness to distort how you see God—how you've kept Him at arm's length. If you don't turn to God now, you might end up falling to Level 3.

Level 3: Reject God as Enemy

The final level of hating God is to flat out reject Him. Satan wants out of God's reality. He wants the power to create his own world apart from God. Fortunately for us, that power is unattainable, and his reign is temporary. He can't escape God's reality, so the best he can accomplish is deceiving others into rejecting God's reality. He knows he can't win, but until God stops him, he'll attempt to move people to despair, weaken their faith, and provoke them to rage against God.

People who hate God have no problem making others suffer. They are caught up in the spirit of evil's ongoing war against God. They've crossed the line from passively ignoring and avoiding God into aggressively seeking to make others suffer too.

People who refuse to give up their bitterness toward God develop three characteristics: a surrender of integrity, a thirst for power, and a hatred for Jesus. As you read about these traits, keep in mind that our struggle isn't against flesh and blood. There's always hope for anyone who would renounce darkness and choose God.

Let's look at three unhealthy ways to express surrender, thirst, and rebellion:

Characteristic #1: A Surrender of Integrity

Everyone has the choice to accept God or reject God. God made us to live for something. Those without something good to live for end up choosing something bad. Without a future beyond this life, what incentive is there to play the long game? Those committed to rejecting God inevitably pursue selfish gain and dishonesty. They open themselves up to all kinds of deception and sin.

A genuine Christian isn't capable of permanently rejecting God. But when a Christian is in touch with his deepest feelings of disappointment in God, he can act from his old self.

Anyone who rejects God must reinvent all that God has already accomplished. Life loses meaning and context. He must determine his own order, structure, and meaning. His moral life is based on his own design, like a fox guarding a hen house. What he lacks in meaning and morals, he makes up for by seizing power.

Characteristic #2: A Thirst for Power

People who hate God lust for power and crave its false promise of control. Sometimes they use it overtly, such as encouraging others to oppress a person or people-group. Other times they adopt a subtler approach, such as deceiving others into distrusting their identity or God's reality.

In the Garden of Eden, Satan promised, *You can become like God.*

"For God knows that when you eat of it your eyes will be opened, and you will be like God, knowing good and evil."
—Genesis 3:5

Notice that Satan never denies God's existence; the best he can do is obscure God's truth. Denying and distorting the truth allows him to subtly redirect people against God. Satan wants to convince us that God shortchanges people and can't be trusted.

Chapter 6 — Overcome Opposition

In order to tempt Jesus, Satan promised Him power and control, with the condition that He switch allegiance from God to Satan.

> *Again, the devil took [Jesus] to a very high mountain and showed him all the kingdoms of the world and their glory. And he said to him, "All these I will give you, if you will fall down and worship me." Then Jesus said to him, "Be gone, Satan! For it is written, "'You shall worship the Lord your God and him only shall you serve.'"*
> —Matthew 4:8–10

Satan wants people to rally against honoring and depending upon God. Many well-intentioned people too easily trade a biblical ideology for another. They lose touch with God's reality. They're deceived into selling out the truth of the Bible, exchanging it for ideas that deface the image of God. They believe lies such as these:

- God wants me to be happy more than He wants me to obey His commands.
- My true identity is a gender different from the one I was born with.
- I can pursue homosexual relationships because God made me with a homosexual orientation.
- I can pursue sexual relationships outside of marriage without consequences.
- Everyone deserves the same benefits and rewards in life regardless of how much or little they work.
- Poor people are lazy; they deserve to suffer.
- Jesus can't be the only way to have eternal life; all religions are essentially the same.

Characteristic #3: A Hatred for Jesus

After someone experiences betrayal and becomes disillusioned with God, that person might be willing to turn against Him and fight for evil. This ultimate rebellion is an aggressive, intentional departure from God's design. Internally, that person will experience Satan's hatred of God and pursue a war against God's design.

God becomes the enemy, and the person in rebellion declares war against Him. The rebel tries to secede and attempts to create a new order. This is what Satan did (see Isaiah 14:12–15).[11] The rebel desires to make life miserable for others, being blinded by a fury of evil like the one that afflicted the people who voted to crucify Jesus.

God has failed us. I don't have the answer, but we can make up our own answer, join together, and fight against the one who is supposed to have the answer. I'll aggressively attempt to destroy God to protest that God passively let me suffer. I want revenge. I want others to suffer if I'm going to suffer. I want to bring pain to God, so I'll strike out against those He cares about.

In the apostle Paul's former life, he opposed Jesus like no other. He killed followers of Jesus. Later, Paul described himself as the "chief of all sinners." He moved against Jesus in self-righteous anger—yet once he realized Jesus was God, he was able to move toward God. God had to ask Paul, "Why are you persecuting me?" and physically blind him to help him see the truth (Acts 9:1–7). Despite Paul's violence against God, God called out to Paul, and Paul became one of Jesus's greatest advocates.

Evil is only possible when God is absent. An empty person who blocks God from her life can only become a magnet for more pain. (Remember how Judas died.) The emptiness and pain motivate stronger resistance against God and encourage an aggressive pursuit of stronger numbing agents. This negative, vicious circle can only end in a bad way unless she involves God again.

If you find yourself hating God but wanting to move toward Him, then confess your need for God and believe in Jesus's death and resurrection. If you're hurt and closed to God so much that you hate Him, you need a strong conversion experience like Paul's.

Bring Your Heart Back to God

When you surrender to disappointment and dethrone God from your life, you also discount your identity. You become lifeless and one-dimensional. You're cemented in hopelessness and focused against God. You're crushed by the weight of guilt and sin, unwilling to receive grace and forgiveness. Fighting against God ultimately defines your existence. Instead of "child of God" you become "enemy of God." Ironically, either way you still define yourself in relationship to God.

Yet there is hope for you; moving against God is moving toward God in many ways. To move against God, you have to acknowledge He exists. An open, angry heart is better than a closed, peaceful one. A truly open-hearted person will naturally move to become allied with God. A closed heart is a hard heart.

A heart polarized against God can more easily flip to offer allegiance to God than an indifferent heart. This happens because God has placed in all of us a desire for connection with Him. This is why I'm a big fan of emotional honesty with God. The more honest you are—even if expressing confused, raging disbelief—the more open your heart will become. If you believe God doesn't want your negative emotions, that He doesn't want to hear how you really feel, you'll close yourself off to God, believing He doesn't care about you and rejects you.

Anger can be healthy. A minor resistance that results in a healthy separation of your identity from God's identity is good. Sometimes you need to step back and fear God. Sometimes God expects us to challenge Him, like when Jacob wrestled with God (Genesis 32) or when Abraham pleaded for Sodom (Genesis 18). As long as you're sincerely embracing your God-given identity and respectfully pursuing God, you can't go wrong.

Fortunately for any Christian, or anyone choosing to become a Christian, the reality is you're allied with God because God paid the price for you in Jesus once for all. Jesus tore down the dividing wall that separates you from God.

The next chapter shows what moving toward God looks like. You can reclaim ground you've lost because of sin, deception, and a hard heart.

Study Questions

1. What parts of your life are in rebellion against God?
2. Create an anger pie-chart. Write the major things you're angry about, along with percentages for each.
3. If you have a bad attitude toward God, how is it distorting your priorities?
4. If you're moving away from God, what level are you at? (Are you ignoring, avoiding, or rejecting God?)
5. What's the farthest you've ever been away from God? If you already know Him, consider the time period since you came to know Him.
6. Can you identify anything that is keeping you away from God? Consider that Jesus died once for all (past, present, and future) sin (Hebrews 10:10, 14, 18).

---

[8] https://www.dictionary.com/browse/disappoint
[9] C. S. Lewis, *The Screwtape Letters* (London: Geoffrey Bles, 1942), Chapter VII.
[10] Consider http://bibleanswerstand.org/why.htm for a more detailed discussion.
[11] http://www.bibletools.org/index.cfm/fuseaction/Topical.show/RTD/cgg/ID/486/Lucifers-Rebellion.htm

Chapter 7

Establish Trust

Every healthy relationship is a two-way street. For you to trust God, you must experience God working for your good. For God to trust you, you must embrace His reality through faith provided by His Holy Spirit living inside you. By sensing God living with you, you're able to know God as good even when life isn't perfect.

Embracing reality means committing to relate to God, creation, and self as God intended so you maximize impact on earth for God's glory and, secondarily, maximize your personal fulfillment.

As you learned in previous chapters, being a Christian doesn't mean you're immune to suffering. But pain without comfort brings despair, not trust, whether you have a relationship with God or not. God may not end your suffering, but He will comfort you. If you can't trust God, you'll miss out on the best part of life—the excitement of experiencing God's kingdom becoming real in you and others.

Faith is the natural expression of trust and the only way to please God. Putting faith in God tells Him, *I trust You. I believe in You. I'm ready to act on my belief.* A person who worries instead of acting in faith is like a dog chasing its tail. There's a lot happening, but not much is accomplished. And a person who claims to have faith but refuses to do anything is equally futile (James 2:17).

Faith is so important to God that it puts you in another category with Him. Believing in God and what He says elevates your status from *servant* to *friend.* As a friend, you're a partner in advancing His kingdom.[12] God makes known His plans so you can be productive.

"You are my friends if you do what I command you. No longer do I call you servants, for the servant does not know what his master is doing;

> *but I have called you friends, for all that I have heard from my Father I have made known to you. You did not choose me, but I chose you and appointed you that you should go and bear fruit and that your fruit should abide, so that whatever you ask the Father in my name, he may give it to you. These things I command you, so that you will love one another."*
> —John 15:14–17

When you open your heart to God and become allied with God, your entire attitude shifts to a faithful optimism. As God's ally, you desire to work alongside God, advancing His kingdom. Your goal is to become a producer, someone who can give back. You recognize and submit to the notion that you live in a reality of God's design. You work diligently to remove obstacles to intimacy with self, God, and others. Instead of resisting God, you cooperate with God and honor the fact that He made everything.

To grow toward your identity, you need God. God is love, and only by receiving His love can you experience acceptance of who you are. I believe Peter was speaking from his experience of denying Christ (John 18:17, 25–27) when he wrote this verse:

> *And after you have suffered a little while, the God of all grace, who has called you to his eternal glory in Christ, will himself restore, confirm, strengthen, and establish you.*
> —1 Peter 5:10

This is good news. God is responsible for helping you grow into your identity. In His grace, He provides the four ingredients needed for your growth and healing.

1. **Restore** means to return to a former condition, place, or position.
2. **Confirm** means to make a public endorsement.
3. **Strengthen** means to support, increase, and reinforce.
4. **Establish** means to bestow permanent acceptance.

Notice the progression. God wants to heal you. First He restores and confirms you. Then He goes on to the unimaginable and strengthens and establishes you. When God establishes you, you have a permanent place in God's kingdom. God has called you to eternal glory. You can't receive a more profound blessing—and it's permanently yours!

Peter experienced God restoring, confirming, strengthening, and establishing him (John 21:15–17). You can, too! This is the work of the Holy Spirit in your life. As you experience regeneration, you can respond by loving God.

The Gentle Climb to Loving God

The path to loving God is a gentle climb in contrast with the slippery slope to hating God. God is gracious and patient with you when you desire to move toward Him. You only need to be facing Him, and you'll have His favor. As you face God, He warms your heart and enables you to respond with greater trust.

> *"Come to me, all who labor and are heavy laden, and I will give you rest. Take my yoke upon you, and learn from me, for I am gentle and lowly in heart, and you will find rest for your souls. For my yoke is easy, and my burden is light."*
> —Matthew 11:28–30

The climb to loving God is a journey that requires playing the long game to finish. To reach the top, you must pass through three steps:

Steps to Loving God	Levels of Trusting God
1: Receive God as Savior	Blind Trust
2: Need God as Lord	Faithful Trust
3: Embrace God as Friend	Established Trust

Step 1: Receive God as Savior

Every baby is born hungry. Similarly, new Christians are eager to learn and grow. They're hungry, enthusiastic, and accepted by God. They need to experience enough acceptance to counter the emotional wounds caused by painful experiences.

A lot of people want to believe an amazing God unconditionally loves them but have a hard time trusting. Maybe that's you. Have you ever wanted to believe what the Bible says about God is true, but you're skeptical because of negative experiences?

You might be thinking, *How can I reconcile my wounding experiences with the truth that God is love? Something is off or missing. Who is God? If He cares, why is He letting me suffer?*

If so, you're not alone, but this could mean you've missed out on receiving enough from God. Receiving God is the easiest step, but we often overlook it because of interference from the curse, sin, and the evil one. If you want to receive God and haven't already done so, see the prayer in Appendix A.

Let's look at three characteristics of people who receive God: hungry, enthusiastic, and accepted.

Characteristic #1: Hungry

A new Christian is eager to learn the basics of the spiritual life.

Like newborn infants, long for the pure spiritual milk, that by it you may grow up into salvation—if indeed you have tasted that the Lord is good.
—1 Peter 2:2–3

Recall from Chapter 5 the story of Mary and Martha. Mary hung on every word of Jesus. She chose to seek directly after God. Jesus reminded Martha that what Mary wanted was good, and it wouldn't be taken away from her. The words of Jesus are life. Jesus is the bread of life that nourishes your spirit (John 6:35).

God conceals valuable truths and reveals them to those who search with a childlike heart. God rewards those who seek.

Chapter 7 — Establish Trust

> *You will seek me and find me,*
> *when you seek me with all your heart.*
> —Jeremiah 29:13

God rewards the persistent and those who boldly ask for what they need (Matthew 15:21–28).

The beginning of a relationship needs intimacy and dialogue to help the relationship grow. Be transparent with God. Ask questions. When calamity struck in Job's life, he had a good reason to be disturbed. He aired out his mind but retained his integrity and respect for God. God showed up and communicated with Job. Like Job, you should pursue God to clear up any misunderstandings.

To depend on God is to put your trust in God and rely on Him. When you do this repeatedly, you're conditioned to depend upon Him. Your dependence becomes a reflex you no longer think about.

Characteristic #2: Enthusiastic

For the new Christian, the contrast of spiritual death and life creates a contagious enthusiasm. We get our word enthusiasm from the Greek *éntheos,* which means "having God within."[13] Jesus compares a first experience of heaven to discovering buried treasure. The kingdom is worth giving up everything you have.

> *"The kingdom of heaven is like treasure hidden*
> *in a field, which a man found and covered up.*
> *Then in his joy he goes and sells all that he has*
> *and buys that field."*
> —Matthew 13:44

The Christian life is easiest when you first find the kingdom. Nothing you did allowed you to earn your way into heaven. So the pressure is off. No performance is necessary. You're forgiven. You're free. You're happy. You're in! You're all in like Peter, who wanted Jesus to wash his whole body, not just his toes.

> *Peter said to him, "You shall never wash my*
> *feet." Jesus answered him, "If I do not wash you,*

> *you have no share with me." Simon Peter said to him, "Lord, not my feet only but also my hands and my head!"*
> —John 13:8–9

Characteristic #3: Accepted

Everybody goes through seasons of realizing they don't know who they are. Everyone feels unworthy, at least occasionally. Being hesitant when facing God is not only normal but can also demonstrate a respectful fear of the Lord. You can wonder, *Will God really accept me after I've done such horrible things?*

Self-doubt is normal. Asking *Who am I?* is normal. What isn't healthy is giving up on finding a better answer today than you had yesterday.

Being accepted means you feel God's unconditional love. Love provides the foundation for security. Jesus is able to completely save the worst of sinners because He always lives to intercede for them (Hebrews 7:25). The truth that Christians can't lose their salvation is a fundamental belief necessary for feeling safe and secure.[14] Because of Jesus, God accepts you with open arms (Hebrews 4:16).

For those locked into seeing God's love as conditional, David Benner, distinguished professor emeritus of psychology and spirituality, describes God's extravagant love:

> *What a different relationship begins to develop when you realize that God is head-over-heals in love with you. God is simply giddy about you. He just can't help loving you. And he loves you deeply, recklessly and extravagantly—just as you are. God knows you are a sinner, but your sins do not surprise him. Nor do they reduce in the slightest his love for you.*[15]

If anyone knew about struggling with self-acceptance, it was the riff-raff of Jesus's day—you know, the sinners—the adulterers and tax collectors. Zacchaeus was a chief tax collector. Tax collectors in those days had the upper hand. Even a Jew would extort as much

Chapter 7 — Establish Trust

money as possible from his fellow Jews. Consequently, Zacchaeus was quite wealthy.

This wealthy man was also quite curious about Jesus. When he heard Jesus was coming to town, he picked out a choice spot. Perhaps you recall the Sunday school song about Zacchaeus being short and needing to climb a tree to see over the crowds.

Much to Zacchaeus's surprise, Jesus singled him out of the crowd and invited Himself to dinner.

> *And when Jesus came to the place,*
> *he looked up and said to him, "Zacchaeus, hurry*
> *and come down, for I must stay at your house*
> *today." So he hurried and came down and*
> *received him joyfully.*
> —Luke 19:5–6

And then, right on the spot, Zacchaeus repented and agreed to pay back any money he had stolen, four times over. What happened? Did Zacchaeus just think quickly and say what he thought would make him look good? No. We know he had a genuine conversion experience.

> *And Jesus said to him, "Today salvation has*
> *come to this house, since he also is a son of*
> *Abraham. For the Son of Man came to seek and*
> *to save the lost."*
> —Luke 19:9–10

Could it be that Jesus's desire to publicly accept and meet with Zacchaeus, a known sinner, was all it took to open Zacchaeus's heart to receiving God? Yes, God's love is incredible, and it sets the foundation for growth.

God initiates your transition to Step 2 by revealing your weaknesses. You become aware of your sin, and consequently, your inability to fix deeper issues or accomplish anything apart from God.

Step 2: Need God as Lord

Every Christian needs God's acceptance, but now I'm talking about *really needing* God. It's the same sort of desperation that comes from walking through a desert for days without any water. After you receive the good news that God loves you and you're going to heaven, God waits a little while before He shares the bad news. Not only are Christians not perfect, they're broken.

You need God to lovingly point out your defects because you can suffer from spiritual blindness. Satan works subtly when he can. The great deceiver whispers, "The path you're on is good enough. You don't need God." Satan is the best salesman. He sold Adam and Eve on choosing hell over God. He sold them on the idea that God was against them, withholding something great. He implied that God lied.

You must make the transition from learning the basics to faithfully living the basics. Faith is easy when life is easy. Receiving God requires little effort on your part, but in order to grow, God expects more from you. You must develop a steadfast belief in God even when all hell breaks loose in your life. You must realize that you need God not just for salvation but for your very next breath. Only God can provide a full understanding of your identity and the path He has for you—and only in His strength can you walk that path.

Hebrews 5:11–6:3 talks about moving on from milk to solid food—being able to discern good from evil, truth from fiction. Your self-image contains lies about you. With God's help, you must sort fact from fiction. Some truths God reveals at the time of His choosing. Other truths are covered by dark, false thoughts that must be exposed and rejected.

Trusting God is nearly impossible if you haven't experienced His blessings. How can you internalize that God is good when crises and negative experiences abound? This is the problem that every believer must resolve. In the midst of pain and suffering, it's difficult to accept that God is good. You need God to help you accept Him in tough times.

If you can't see God as good, seek God. Talk to Him. Tell Him about your doubts and pain. Wrestle with Him like Job did. You need God especially in the painful times. Just know that there is nowhere else to turn. God is the creator and sustainer of the universe. He is all-good and all-knowing. There is none like Him.

God is either all-good, or He's got some bad in Him. If He's got some bad, He's not perfect. How then could you trust Him? Life is hopeless without God's perfect goodness. Should you ever start to believe you can't safely embrace God—like Adam and Eve who slipped into doubting God and believing Satan—realize you're about to give up on the best and only option for an abundant life.

Christians who have grown through several seasons of suffering and deeply experienced their need for God are faithful, repentant, and humble. Let's look at these characteristics more closely.

Characteristic #1: Faithful

Ironically, the way God demonstrates His goodness is to bring trials into your life. Trials help you discover your identity. God is smart. He excels at accomplishing multiple things at the same time. While you're suffering, He can both help you grow and show you how good He is.

During trials, He asks you to trust Him more and not necessarily make sense of everything. Some things God keeps hidden. This encourages you to develop your faith muscle. If everything were easy, you wouldn't have to trust and rely on God.

What does having a faithful heart mean? Every step of Abraham's life required clinging to God's promises in spite of the lack of evidence. He constantly had to overlook the negative interpretation of his circumstances and trust what God told him. Abraham had faithful trust because he listened to God and believed Him. He chose to emphasize God's voice over his circumstances. Over the course of his life, Abraham

- left the land where he grew up and moved to an unknown land,
- allowed his nephew to choose the more fertile land while he took the less fertile land,
- believed God would provide a son through his wife even when she was too old to conceive, and

- trusted God would provide a way forward even if he sacrificed his son.

God's promises were enough to keep Abraham moving forward. The faithful believe despite contrary evidence. A faithful heart relies on God despite what it experiences. Abraham believed God; God counted Abraham as a friend (James 2:23).

Characteristic #2: Repentant

One way to obey God is through prayer and repentance. When you spend time with God in prayer, He opens your mind and pours in wisdom. This leads to maturity and an acceptance of His will, even when it doesn't make sense.

Repentance is trusting in God's righteousness, not your own. True repentance isn't just saying you're sorry. Repentance requires admitting vulnerability. You realize how you royally messed up and have no way to fix the problem. If you want out of the hole you've dug, humility is your only option. You *really* need God.

Christian author Bill Thrall emphasizes that you can't dig yourself out of your hole by willpower:

> *Repentance is about trusting, not willing.*
> *Repentance isn't doing something about our sin;*
> *rather, it means admitting we can't do anything*
> *about our sin.*[16]

By repenting, you bring yourself into alignment with God's intentions for your life. You believe in an absolute truth. You surrender to God's way and admit dependence upon Him. You take seriously that God has real intentions for how to live, and you respond with your commitment to live this way.

David became arrogant and didn't go to war alongside his soldiers, and it led him to sin. When he was called out by Nathan, his repentance was genuine. David wasn't perfect, but when confronted with the truth, he aligned with it and pressed forward without hesitation.

He was a man after God's own heart and a mature follower of God. He cared more about his reputation in God's eyes than in the eyes of the public. He was willing to look silly in front of others. He didn't care what others thought about him as he worshipped God (see 2 Samuel 6).

The most sophisticated method of coping is to grow beyond the problem. The problem shrinks relative to your maturity. You begin to see your need for God by noticing how messed up you are. You admit it freely and recognize that you desperately need to experience His forgiveness.

Characteristic #3: Humble

Moses represented all of Israel to God. He humbly served others, interceded like a priest, and often saved the immature, sinful Israelites from God's holiness.

Moses was so humble that God related to him in a more intimate way than He did with any other people of that time.

> *Now the man Moses was very meek, more than all people who were on the face of the earth. [The Lord said,] "He is faithful in all my house. With him I speak mouth to mouth, clearly, and not in riddles, and he beholds the form of the LORD."*
> —Numbers 12:3, 7b, 8a

Moses didn't always agree with God. In fact, when God chose him to lead the Israelites out of Egypt, he trembled with fear and refused God. In a sense, he was too humble. God was angry with him for not being willing to confront his fears and fulfill God's plan to rescue the Israelites.

Moses had some growing to do before he became a great leader. Fortunately for him, God knew who he really was. God knew his true identity, while all Moses had was his self-image. Moses needed faith to grow toward his identity.

A humble heart continues to obey and depend on God despite disagreement. A humble heart trusts and respects God. What naturally follows is surrender and submission. You adjust yourself to God rather than expecting God to adjust to you. You see this as a good thing. You appreciate the safety of God's reality.

The Israelites frequently rebelled against God. They created a golden calf when Moses was away. Moses often pleaded with God to have mercy on His people. He obeyed God but also interceded for his fellow Israelites when they acted foolishly (see Exodus 32).

When you have received God and realize how much you need God, you also realize there is a healthy way to rebel. Healthy rebellion means separating from worldly wisdom to find a deeper meaning in life—you connect face-to-face with your Creator.

God initiates your transition to Step 3 by calling you to a ministry beyond the scope of your day-to-day life. This typically happens when your fear is replaced by faithfulness. Unfortunately, there's no short cut; Moses endured the desert for forty years. But once you realize how much your trials have strengthened your faith, your focus can shift from surviving life to identifying the best way to advance God's kingdom.

Step 3: Embrace God as Friend

Trials establish your trust in God as you ultimately see Him working for the good of His people. As you grow in faithfulness, you can truly love God. You can love God because He loved you first (1 John 4:19). Embracing God is the final step toward God because love requires you to give all you have—heart, soul, strength, and mind (Luke 10:27). Your faith is mature (James 1:1–4). Having survived the desperation of needing God, and having learned over time to remain in His presence, you understand that you may have to accept many defeats before victory comes. But victory is guaranteed.

For victory in life, we've got to keep focused on the goal, and the goal is Heaven.
—Lou Holtz

What is your experience with trust? You probably trust your chair to hold you. Would you trust a pilot to fly you twenty miles above the ground in a plane weighing nearly one million pounds? If we can trust a pilot with our lives, how much more can we trust the God who makes and sustains all things?

Loving God requires giving all you've got, including your identity—everything He's made you to be. It's possible only because God gave all He had. Carl Jung summarized what is required to love God:

> *[Loving God] demands unconditional trust and expects absolute surrender. Just as nobody but the believer who surrenders himself wholly to God can partake of divine grace, so love reveals its highest mysteries and its wonder only to those who are capable of unqualified devotion.*[17]

When you love God with abandon, your faith is unstoppable and you trust God will complete the work He's started in you (Philippians 1:6). You love others, sacrifice for them, and defend their freedoms. You see life beyond the curse and despair on earth. This gives you hope to keep going. You have an unshakeable hope because your faith allows you to see beyond what is immediately in front of you.

Someone who loves God is disciplined, courageous, and sacrificial. Let's look at these characteristics more closely.

Characteristic #1: Disciplined

For God to love us, He must give all He is, holding nothing back. To love God is to fully receive all He is and offer our devotion to His cause—that is, His kingdom. Accomplishing this requires discipline and focus, because, as we learned in Chapter 6, distractions, obstacles, and negative circumstances exist to stop you.

Paul was disciplined. He devoted himself completely to the cause of advancing God's kingdom. God revealed heaven to him, and he tasted it (2 Corinthians 12:2). Once you see heaven, losing sight of its glory is impossible.

> *Brothers, I do not consider that I have made it my own. But one thing I do: forgetting what lies*

> *behind and straining forward to what lies ahead,*
> *I press on toward the goal for the prize of the*
> *upward call of God in Christ Jesus.*
> *I have become all things to all people, that by all*
> *means I might save some. I do it all for the sake*
> *of the gospel, that I may share with them in its*
> *blessings. Do you not know that in a race all the*
> *runners run, but only one receives the prize? So*
> *run that you may obtain it. Every athlete*
> *exercises self-control in all things. They do it to*
> *receive a perishable wreath, but we an*
> *imperishable. So I do not run aimlessly; I do not*
> *box as one beating the air. But I discipline my*
> *body and keep it under control,*
> *lest after preaching to others*
> *I myself should be disqualified.*
> —Philippians 3:13–14; 1 Corinthians 9:22b–27

Characteristic #2: Courageous

In order to grow, you have to risk. But the risk is reasonable because God has proven Himself faithful time and again. His perfect love drives out fear (1 John 4:18). A confident heart is courageous and presses forward in faith despite the odds.

Joshua's story is an example of courageously loving God in contrast with those who lack faith. Joshua saw all that God did to deliver the Israelites from evil. Despite the hardship of slavery and the difficulty of the journey through the desert, he emphasized God's goodness. He served God in sincerity and faithfulness and prompted the Israelites to do the same (Joshua 24:14–15).

Moments after Joshua's declaration of faith, the rest of Israel joined him in declaring their allegiance to God. The people pledged before God the same oath that Joshua swore (Joshua 24:16–18). However, we also know from Judges 2 that the majority of people eventually gave up on God. Their sincerity wasn't good enough. Let's be honest: they were great at faking sincerity. Or perhaps they didn't really know what they were getting themselves into. Later they either forgot about God's goodness or no longer counted God's faithfulness as good enough. They abandoned God to follow other gods and engage in evil practices.

The Israelites started with enthusiasm and ended with broken promises. They failed to understand the effort required to finish what they started.[18] Courage without perseverance is immature at best and constitutes hypocrisy at worst.

> *"Whoever does not bear his own cross and come after me cannot be my disciple. For which of you, desiring to build a tower, does not first sit down and count the cost, whether he has enough to complete it? Otherwise, when he has laid a foundation and is not able to finish, all who see it begin to mock him, saying, 'This man began to build and was not able to finish.'"*
> —Luke 14:27–30

Winston Churchill, British Prime Minister during World War II, changed history with his courageous optimism in the face of evil. He helped keep a frightened nation focused against all odds. Because he didn't give up, Hitler's Germany didn't win.

> *You have enemies? Good. That means you've stood up for something, sometime in your life. Things are not always right because they are hard, but if they are right one must not mind if they are also hard. If you're going through hell, keep going. Never give in, never give in, never, never, never, never—in nothing, great or small, large or petty—never give in except to convictions of honor and good sense.*
> —Winston Churchill

You need courage to maintain your convictions. If your goal is noble, pursue it despite the odds. If you don't give up, you can't fail.

In the Parable of the Talents (Matthew 25:14–30), the master gave talents (money) to three of his servants according to their ability. Two of the servants used their God-given resources without hesitation even though significant risk was involved. The master showered them with equal praise, independent of their ability.

> *"Well done, good and faithful servant. You have been faithful over a little; I will set you over much. Enter into the joy of your master."*
> —Matthew 25:23

The third servant was frozen in fear and merely hoarded his master's resources. The master's offer of talents demonstrated his confidence in the servant, a trust that was violated. Because God has invested His love in us, we can be faithful stewards and take risks for God's kingdom.

Characteristic #3: Sacrificial

Someone at this stage in her spiritual journey has tasted enough of God's goodness that she can freely surrender immediate gain for the sake of participating in the fulfillment of God's kingdom (Hebrews 11:24–26).

Jesus has a perfect relationship with God; therefore, He is the best example of loving God completely. He defined maximum love as being willing to sacrifice your life for those you care about.

> *"This is my commandment, that you love one another as I have loved you. Greater love has no one than this, that someone lay down his life for his friends."*
> —John 15:12–13

Jesus is fully human in every way (Hebrews 2:17). Before He willingly died on the cross for us, He revealed His humanity at Gethsemane. He had His best friends (Peter, James, and John) with Him and desired their companionship. Despite being in great distress over His anticipated death, He couldn't stop thinking about how this would impact His friends. He wanted His friends to be safe. So He told them to stay alert to avoid temptation.

Chapter 7 — Establish Trust

Jesus didn't want to experience betrayal and a painful death. He expressed His desire to avoid the crucifixion even though He had to have known there was no other way. He pleaded with the Father for another way. He acknowledged God could ease His pain, but equally surrendered to the Father's greater purposes. He genuinely appealed to God, knowing that with God all things are possible. His desire to avoid pain was only surpassed by His desire to stay in tune with God's reality. His spirit was willing, but in His humanity He didn't want to experience the agony. Jesus's desire to avoid painful circumstances are no different than yours or mine—except that He always stayed the course and finished what God said was best (Mark 14:32–38).

Sacrifice can be profound and final like Jesus's crucifixion. But sacrifice is just as real, if not more so, when it is daily, bite-sized, and ongoing. You can lay down your life by spending time with your children when you can think of more interesting things to do, by providing for your family when you don't like your job, or by serving others on the other side of your city or the other side of the world.

Embracing God as friend is possible because of the mutual investment you and God have made in developing an intimate relationship. God is always friendly toward you because of Jesus's sacrifice, but a friendship develops and deepens only with time and trust.

God played the long game by sending Jesus to die for us. Jesus leads by example. He didn't want to die, but He trusted God to make the right decision. And now His rule has only just begun.

The tyrant dies and his rule is over,
the martyr dies and his rule begins.
—Soren Kierkegaard

Choose Life or Death

Joshua was able to choose life. I trust you want this too. In order to choose life, you must evaluate your self-image. When you lack

awareness of your true identity, your self-image keeps you immature and D.E.A.D. As long as you maintain this false identity, you will
- **Deviate** from God's design by disguising your true identity, removing it from awareness, or never seeking it out;
- **Elevate** some aspect of creation above God's intentions;
- **Approve** of your self-image when it contradicts your God-given identity; and
- **Destroy** the harmony between internal identity (your self-image), external identity (both your behaviors and how others see you), and God's design (your true identity).

When you cultivate a true, confident identity that is A.L.I.V.E., you will:
- **Achieve** awareness of who you are and who you aren't;
- **Live** with and seek after God's design;
- **Identify** God as your source of primary fulfillment, only relying on creation as a secondary resource as God intended;
- **Value** life as it is by accepting both the happiness of knowing your true self and the suffering caused by evil; and
- **Encourage** the harmony between internal identity, external identity, and God's design.

Every life has a crossover point—when a person is able to consistently produce more fruit than he needs to consume. During Part III of this book, I'll show you the normal stages you'll go through as you pursue your identity. But first, in Part II, I want to help you get in touch with your journey by witnessing others' journeys.

Chapter 7 — Establish Trust

Study Questions

1. Where are you at in your gentle climb to loving God?
2. How desperate is your pursuit of God?
3. Review the Window of Optimal Comfort diagram in Chapter 6. What obstacles have you encountered in your gentle climb to God?
4. Read Hebrews 4:14–16. Do you believe Jesus knows what it's like to genuinely struggle with suffering and pain?
5. Read Hebrews 7:24–25. How does Jesus's availability to always intercede for you affect your sense of security?
6. In what ways are you struggling to accept God's will for your life?
7. How much harmony do you experience between your self-image and your identity?
8. Have you accepted the fact that there are no short cuts to loving God? Are you able to enjoy where you're at in the journey?

---

[12] https://bible.org/seriespage/lesson-37-friendship-god-genesis-181-8
[13] https://www.dictionary.com/browse/enthusiasm
[14] God gives you eternal life by faith and your belief is what keeps you eternally secure. After you become a Christian, be careful to interpret the Bible as one who is God's child. When you believe you gain eternal life, not temporary life (see John 3:16, Ephesians 2:8–9, 1 John 5:10–21). You can safely ignore condemning verses because God intends these for the non-Christian (see Romans 8, Hebrews 7:24–25; 10:39; 12:3).
[15] David G. Benner, *Surrender to Love* (Downers Grove: Intervarsity Press, 2003), p.18.
[16] Bill Thrall, *TrueFaced* (Colorado Springs: NavPress, 2004), p. 103, 116.
[17] Carl Jung, *Aspects of the Masculine* (Princeton, N.J.: Princeton University Press, 1989), p. 59.
[18] To better understand, also consider the Parable of the Sower in Matthew 13. The Israelites are like the rocky or thorny soil.

Part II — Journey to Identity

Chapter 8   **Andrew's Journey**

Chapter 9   **Samantha's Journey**

Chapter 10   **Olivia's Journey**

Let's look at three people to see some examples of navigating life to find identity. Andrew struggles at first to understand who he is, but his encounters with reality and becoming a Christian help him mature. Samantha becomes a Christian too but can't overcome her past, move beyond her crisis, and become calling focused. Olivia is creation focused and struggles to find success and fulfillment. She fails to see God during the crisis points in her life, so she refocuses on creation and looks for comfort there.

Chapter 8

Andrew's Journey

Andrew was born into a dysfunctional family dynamic. His sister Emily, three years older, had already developed a special attachment to her father. Emily's mother loved her but felt out of place and unfulfilled as a mother. The frustration impacted the marriage and ultimately led her to favor Andrew.

As Andrew grew up, whenever he would mess up, his mother was quick to shield him from negative consequences. She couldn't bear to see her son look bad compared to Emily—who like her father was an academic achiever. Andrew lacked a sense of who he was beyond being a recipient of his mom's caregiving.

My mom always helps me get what I want. If I want to do or have something, I need my mom.

Andrew enjoyed solitary activities and therefore kept to himself most of the time. His mom encouraged him to develop friends and often took him to playdates. While over at friends' houses, he gravitated toward toys he didn't have at home—especially the electronics.

Andrew would throw a fit when he had to stop playing a computer game and couldn't take it home with him. His mom would purchase the game, often on the way home, even if she had to give up something she wanted. His dad enjoyed his job, but money was tight.

In school, Andrew didn't get along with the smart kids (who were too much like his sister), but neither did he fit in with the athletes. He lacked motivation to try much of anything. His sister benefited from choosing a direction. Her dad spent a lot of time with her focused on their common interests. When Andrew's dad gave Emily $150 to spend on a science project, Andrew's mom made sure he also received $150. With his mom's help, Andrew picked out a new bicycle—and had enough money left over for a new computer game and several comic books.

TO IDENTITY AND BEYOND

When a dad isn't there for a boy and he is coddled by his mom, he becomes emasculated and his self-image is fractured. He feels lost and hopeless.

I can't compare to my sister. My mom says it's okay I'm different. I should be able to enjoy myself instead of working so hard like my sister.

Emily found a self-image she could start developing. She was well on her way to growing up with a confident identity. Andrew was more laid-back than his sister. God designed him this way, but Andrew lacked the sense of who he was. God wants everyone, including more laid-back personalities, to feel sure of who they are.

Andrew favored his mom, and he learned to feel insecure about himself because of her over-involvement. The lack of attention from his dad wasn't intentional, but it was damaging. His dad loved him, but they didn't connect around anything. Andrew's parents couldn't tell him who he was, so how could he know who he was?

Andrew spent hours playing video games. He grew older on the outside but remained a young child on the inside. He lacked motivation for school. Even though he failed English, his mom convinced the school to promote him by assuring the principal she would catch him up over the summer.

I love playing games, but my grades suck. No worries, though. Mom is taking care of the school—making sure I move to the next grade along with my friends. But where do I fit in?

When his dad tried to redirect him to take more responsibility, his mom intervened by insisting they couldn't expect Andrew to be like his sister. This helpful intention eventually created significant tension in the family, which only further isolated Andrew.

Mom takes care of me, but I wish Dad would notice me more. I'm not sure who I am. I'm confused. Why do I get along better with my mom?

Andrew's game worlds became more real to him than his real life. He was more successful in them than he ever was in school. His virtual friends became more important than his in-person friends. But he stayed in touch with one in-person friend, Mark, through high school.

Chapter 8 — Andrew's Journey

My online friends understand me better than anyone. I really like Mark, though. I wish he liked playing computer games.

Mark played soccer and invited Andrew to join his team. Much to his parents' surprise, Andrew showed interest in playing soccer. He wasn't the best player on the team, but he found he had some talent for sports after all. His mom, of course, attended all his games, while his dad made it to a couple of games a season. Andrew practiced his skills some, but whenever Mark spent time with his girlfriend, Andrew spent the rest of his free time immersed in video games.

Mark is dating already, but I'm not that interested in girls. I like that I have soccer—something I'm sort of good at besides computer games. Games are still my favorite, though.

By the time he graduated high school, he'd had enough of school, so he opted out of college. When he turned eighteen, he started smoking and stopped playing soccer. Meanwhile, Emily graduated college early.

Andrew continued to live at home while he worked at a local grocery store and spent all his money on games, comics, junk food, and cigarettes. His parents paid for his car insurance, and often gas and maintenance too. His mom didn't want him smoking but couldn't bring herself to deny her son any of life's pleasures. He was already suffering, she mused. How could she remove something that kept him motivated in some way?

I don't have a real job, but who cares? Mom takes care of me. She gets me what I want and keeps the fridge filled with the food I like. I'm happy when I'm playing my games. I don't have to worry about what to do with my life.

Andrew dated a few different girls. This only happened when the girl asked him out. The relationships never went anywhere because he didn't feel any sense of what to do next. When a girl stopped calling, he never followed up with her, reasoning that she didn't like him. He didn't know what to do—he was so used to his mom doing everything for him.

Andrew became so immersed in video games that he frequently stayed up playing until six in the morning. At first, he only did this on the weekends, but eventually he did this on work nights. He showed up for work late a couple of times a month. One day, he slept in too long, didn't make it into work at all, and lost his job.

I can get another job, no problem. Video games are fun. I wish the video game world was my real life. I'll never accomplish as much my superstar sister. She is married now. Good for her, but I can't imagine that for me.

His dad, hoping to spark some ambition in him, said he'd have to move into the basement if he wanted to keep living at home—and he'd have to start paying rent. But his mom insisted he shouldn't have to pay rent. Andrew wasn't wild about the basement, but it still beat the alternative of facing the challenges of the real world.

Andrew continued to be a loner. All he knew growing up was his mom's identity—her caring presence. He was as much his mom's son as he was his own person. Andrew was physically mature but emotionally and spiritually immature.

I live in my parents' basement—so what? My mom still gives me money so I can buy my cigarettes and play the games I want. But she feels too close to me sometimes. I wish someone other than her would take a real interest in my life. I'll find another job eventually. I wonder how long I'll be living with my parents.

Andrew's parents' marriage reached a boiling point. They attended marriage counseling and worked out their different parenting styles. His mom attended some individual counseling and found her own identity apart from being a mother. She started realizing how much she was holding back her son.

To grow, Andrew needed to desire to separate from his mom—to rebel in some healthy way so he could accept more responsibility for his life. His mom engaged in tough love by encouraging him to leave the nest. He looked for a job more seriously and took the first one he could find.

Andrew sensed a real change in his situation. One of his coworkers invited him to church. Andrew ventured out and accepted the invitation. Even though he made a profession of faith in Jesus Christ and joined the church, he continued to feel isolated. At least his church fed him spiritually.

Andrew's dad took a more direct interest in him. Andrew started to feel good about his relationship with his dad—and then suddenly

Chapter 8 — Andrew's Journey

his parents sat him down. Together, they told him it was time for him to leave the house.

Andrew moved out three weeks later. He worked hard to pay his bills. He wasn't used to the extra work and often came home exhausted. However, despite being tired, he felt motivated to thrive like he'd never felt before.

I have no time to enjoy life. Now even my mom is pushing me away. Allowing her to be too close only delayed me growing up. My dad is more interested, but he still doesn't get me. I still don't get me. I don't have anything to give to others. I wish I had been exposed to more experiences growing up. My mom made my life easy, but I'm paying for it now. I wonder why my sister never had this problem. I'll never be like her, but I need to figure out how to make my life work.

Andrew felt the emptiness of his life for the first time and hungered to make sense of his life. The next year appeared to produce little change. However, being forced to take care of himself more than he ever had before also forced him to seriously consider what he wanted from life.

There is a lot more to life than playing video games and smoking. I've lost ten years of my life; I'm 25 but feel like I'm 15. I've got a lot of catching up to do. If mom hadn't changed, I bet I'd still be living in my parent's basement playing video games all day and night.

When Andrew considered how numb he'd been, all he could do was stare at his bedroom wall. He felt as confused as ever but more alive than ever. Andrew enrolled in school, deciding to pursue his love of comic books by training to be a graphic designer. He continued to work physical labor jobs to pay his bills while attending school.

He accepted some financial help from his parents. They agreed to help him because he had taken the initiative to pursue school without their prodding.

Andrew graduated with an associate degree in graphic design. This helped him find a better job, but this didn't fix how he felt about himself.

Not only did Andrew not know how to relate to God, he lacked the ability to express emotions and connect to others. He didn't see himself as having anything that could ever be of value to anyone. This came across to the women he tried to date. He took the initiative to ask out a few women, but they quickly decided to end the relationship.

I'm unwanted by everyone except my mom. I'm learning about the Bible at my church, but I feel like something is missing. I feel dead inside. My social life feels like a dead end. I'm restless. I told mom. Even though she seemed to care, she didn't jump in and help me like she used to. I need to take action to move forward in life.

Andrew looked for a different church with a healthy group of people in their twenties. He participated in as many activities as he could. He made a couple of friends and enjoyed relationships at a deeper level than he had ever experienced. They would go to the movies, go hiking, and play soccer. Until now, enjoying relationships was nearly impossible. He could enjoy receiving from others, but enjoying mutual give-and-take was something different altogether.

Being a Christian is opening up a whole new dimension in my life. I finally have some hope that life will be much better than it has been. I sense God cares about me. I finally know what it's like to feel accepted and secure—but I'm still unclear on who I am and what to do with my life.

Andrew began attending a Bible study with his friends. He went on a spiritual retreat that further accelerated his growth. He found a connection with an older man that could mentor him.

Feeling I have something to offer others is amazing. I love my life now. My life is a real adventure. I still like playing video games, but I want to invest more into the adventure God has planned for me. Life is about something totally different than I experienced growing up.

So many good things happened that he could attribute to God. He felt like he was waking up from a bad dream. He felt disoriented and excited about life at the same time.

Chapter 8 — Andrew's Journey

Andrew earned a bachelor's degree and found a woman he wanted to pursue. He had come a long way in five years. A whole new adventure was ahead of him: he married and had children.

God has truly blessed me, and I'm going to make a good life for myself and my family. I sense God has something more planned for me.

Over the next ten years, God showed Andrew hints of his identity, and this helped him correct his self-image from "hopeless dependent" to "son of God" to "significant contributor." He learned how to disciple others and has now started a discipleship ministry at his church. God now regularly sends people Andrew's way for a period of healing before sending them out again into the world.

I have my struggles in life like everyone else, but my hope in You isn't in vain. I sense You are with me. My identity comes from You, God. No one can take it from me! No one can take me away from You! I belong to You. I need to continue to mature, but nothing's going to keep me from Your love.

I've found my calling and purpose. Your glory is my focus. I take pleasure in doing my part. I'm hopeful as You fulfill Your plans. I'm gifted in helping others experience Your truth. I'm making a difference advancing God's kingdom one person at a time.

Study Questions

1. What prevented Andrew from growing up sooner?
2. What was the turning point in Andrew's life?
3. What was Andrew's self-image before and after the turning point?
4. Can you relate to Andrew in any way? If so, how?

Chapter 9

Samantha's Journey

You're already familiar with Samantha from Chapter 6. She became a Christian, but her negative life experiences prevented her from fully resolving her crisis.

Her mom and dad were always fighting about something. Her mom would even yell at the top of her lungs and sometimes hit her dad. Samantha tried to make them calm down and stop. Half the time her mom would yell at her too.

The family dealt with these blow-ups by not talking about them. Instead, they spent money to have fun. They went out to eat multiple times a week and frequently went to amusement parks, sporting events, and the movie theater.

Her mom dropped her off at church each week. Samantha enjoyed the social aspect. Her youth pastor noticed her organizational ability and asked her to help with youth event details.

Samantha's parents didn't mature and ended up divorced when she was thirteen. They explained that she would live with her mom, but her dad promised to spend time with her every week. She blamed her mom, held anger toward her, and saw her as hypocritical for divorcing her dad.

Samantha and her mom had a lot of conflict. Her mom lost interest in church and stopped taking her to church. Samantha couldn't feel good about herself, so she couldn't feel close to God.

Samantha's dad didn't yell at her, but he didn't call her either. In fact, he never showed up for their scheduled time. There were no acute traumas to overlook, but the neglect harmed her all the same. Samantha didn't have the opportunity to say, *Dad, I'm disappointed you didn't keep your promise.*

When Samantha looks back on her childhood, she feels guilty. *I have no reason to feel so sad. I should be thankful I wasn't abused. I had a normal, good childhood.*

Samantha can disconnect from reality by insisting her childhood was better than what she actually experienced. People do this all the time as a way to avoid the pain of neglect or abuse.

Samantha became a Christian during a church event right after she graduated from high school. A couple of her friends celebrated with her. Unfortunately, the high point of her life was swiftly overshadowed by tragedy: a week after her conversion, she was date-raped by a guy she had just started seeing. She felt ashamed and didn't tell anyone.

Samantha's self-image suffered, and so did her view of God. The passage of time didn't heal anything. When she reached the age of 24, the pain was still unbearable. Samantha thought, *If God is good, why do I suffer and despise my life? Why, like Job, do I wish I was never born? What good is there in being a Christian? Why did God let my parents divorce? Why did He allow me to be raped? Why did I agree to that date?*

To resolve her confusion, she attempted a compromise. She wouldn't let go of her belief in God, but she reserved the right to stay angry at Him. She wouldn't reject God altogether, but she couldn't trust Him anymore than she could trust her parents. This lack of trust caused her to drift away from God.

Samantha's felt experience of abandonment didn't match God's promise, *I'll never leave you.* She felt trapped in a reality she didn't understand. She had experienced too much suffering, but not enough positive experience with God.

I think God is real, but at the same time, I'm in too much pain for God to be real. I don't know how to stop feeling so terrible.

In her suffering, she formed a negative view of God. She doubted God cared and saw Him as uninvolved and unreachable. Distrusting God made sense to her because she hadn't experienced enough good things in life. She relied heavily on creation instead of God. She began a vicious cycle of binging and purging her food.

Samantha neither denied God nor pursued Him. She accepted the benefits of eternal life, but her anger prevented intimacy with a God who had betrayed her. Holding on in this way kept her brokenness hidden from her own eyes.

Chapter 9 — Samantha's Journey

Samantha became disconnected from and out of touch with reality. Her heartbreak resulted in low self-esteem. She remained hard on the outside but tender and fragile underneath. *God, why would You save me only to let me be raped a week later? Nothing is going my way. No one is ever going to like me. No one is going to want me now. God, I feel so alone.*

Unable to worship God, she fixated on the world around her instead. Like her mother, she distanced herself from her faith. She didn't want to face how she really felt about herself. She couldn't see a positive self-image. She acted on impulse, using creation to satisfy her physical and relational desires, adopting a promiscuous lifestyle while her bulimic struggles continued. She felt intense shame and longed for happiness. All of this helped her avoid finding a real answer to the difficult question, *How can God be good if life is so full of suffering?*

Samantha became so angry at God that she decided she would rather live bitter and away from God than in relationship with the God who allowed her to suffer. She focused on her desire to feel relationally fulfilled by dating several men. But she couldn't find anyone who could love her like she wanted to be loved. She caught one of them cheating on her, and the others were too preoccupied with their own interests, which only aggravated her sense of abandonment.

God could stop the pain, but He won't. I hate God so much that I'd rather be away from God in hell than at God's side in heaven.

Samantha's crisis level peaked, and she struggled with suicidal thoughts. Because she could feel the pain, she was closer to moving beyond the crisis. Samantha's thoughts continued to plague her, and she couldn't escape the despair, but hitting bottom helped her reach out to God. Instead of choosing suicide, she decided to return to church to give God another chance. In the church service, she felt a tugging from God, so she began to seek Him again.

The Bible says You'll never leave or forsake me. Why do I feel abandoned, then? What am I missing, God? I don't know if I'll ever feel any different, but I need to try something.

When Samantha couldn't trust God, she linked her sense of security to her feelings. She felt her life was intolerably out of control. What Samantha desired on the surface—a perfect relationship with a man—was a malfunctioning desire. She used creation in ways God never intended. She couldn't control how other men saw her. But she could learn more about her longings for security that God had placed in her heart.

Samantha's friend, Sarah, reminded her of her organizational gifts. Samantha decided to volunteer as a coordinator for the youth ministry. She showed up at the next event to help, but it didn't seem like she was needed. She went home vowing to never volunteer again.

Sarah had another idea, encouraging Samantha to join a codependency group. *At least Sarah hasn't abandoned me. She's so encouraging.* The group called her out when she attempted to avoid her feelings by focusing on taking care of others. At first, Samantha didn't like this and pushed back, but in time she dropped her guard enough to stop feeling so alone and start learning more about her identity.

Her pastor, quoting from Psalm 139, explained God's intimate and intentional involvement in creating her. "For You created my inmost being; You knit me together in my mother's womb. I praise You because I am fearfully and wonderfully made; Your works are wonderful, I know that full well."

God, You must have a purpose for me. I just wish I knew what it was. I wish I could feel close to You.

As Samantha pursued her healing in the weeks that followed, she prayed more than she used to. She tentatively accepted her recent positive experiences with God but remained skeptical that He wouldn't let her down again. Her understanding of her self-image and identity started to become more positive, but her worldview remained tainted with a negative attitude toward God.

Samantha grieved over her mistakes and lamented her feelings of inadequacy, but her anxiety and frustration seemed endless.

I long to feel loved. God, why won't You let me feel close to You? You're so distant and uncaring. Not only did my parents' marriage fail, but so did all of my relationships. Why do I attract the wrong men? There's no hope I'll ever get better. Where were my parents?

Chapter 9 — Samantha's Journey

Where were You? Why is food so important to me? I failed at everything!

Samantha wasn't able to trust God for positive outcomes in her life. Instead, she remained consumed with her own pain, unable to see past it.

The Bible says You love me, but I don't feel loved. I'm worthless. The lies are too real. I don't know how to trust. My parents weren't there for me. My boyfriend cheated on me. You're supposed to care, but instead You abandoned me! How will I ever be able to trust?

Samantha was vulnerable to taking on life's problems *as* her identity. She didn't make enough progress in understanding her identity to see beyond herself into God's spiritual realm. God blessed her, but she remained self-focused, unable to stop obsessing over her emotional wounds.

Instead of making peace with God, she devoted herself to medical school. As a doctor, she over-functioned in her patient's lives, becoming frustrated when they didn't follow her instructions.

She met a man where she worked. He said he was a Christian, and they didn't wait long to get married. She looked to him to provide for her, and though he was a good man, he fell short in many ways. He was stable but passive. She craved a deeper relationship.

When Samantha felt especially threatened, she would hit her husband. She couldn't manage her primal emotional needs, so she erupted in anger instead. Her experience of her emptiness would overwhelm her before she could really understand what she needed. Her desire for security was good and proper, but the demands she placed on her husband were inappropriate.

I wish I could wake up feeling close to God instead of this dreadful emptiness. Why are others so happy? Why are You so close to them? I don't know what to do with my loneliness except eat until the pain is gone.

Samantha continues to limp along in life. She has never lost the sense that God is keeping His distance, even though she can see God working in the lives of other people around her. She frequently uses food to soothe her distress. She trusts God for salvation but is unable to trust Him for anything more, focusing too much on how she feels.

Study Questions

1. What prevented Samantha from moving past her crisis?
2. What evidence is there that Samantha is a Christian?
3. Describe Samantha's self-image.
4. Can you relate to Samantha in any way? If so, how?

Chapter 10

Olivia's Journey

Olivia's life had a happy beginning. After she was born, her mom was able to stop working to stay home with her. Her mom took her to the park and other fun activities, including preschool. Olivia loved being around other children. Every year after she turned three, she and her family took a long summer vacation.

Life is fun. I like people. I love my parents.

When Olivia was only seven years old, she started taking piano lessons and showed real talent. Her instructor commented that she was a real performer. That same year, her mother decided to return to work. This meant staying at a friend's house after school until her mom came home.

Olivia felt the abrupt change and missed her mom, but she enjoyed spending time with her neighborhood friend. This turned out to be a win-win—until her friend's older brother started touching her inappropriately. Olivia kept this a secret for two years. When she finally found the courage to tell her mom, her mom said she was old enough to be home alone, but downplayed the significance of the abuse. Olivia felt like her mom didn't believe her.

I can't trust people to keep me safe and provide what I need. I need to manage my own life.

When Olivia socialized, she kept the hurt parts of herself safely tucked away. Her piano instructor noticed a change and commented to her mom that she had become less expressive. Overall, school was a positive for her. She developed several friendships but she kept them at arm's length. She maintained a love-hate relationship with school. She was quite capable, but also quite distracted.

Olivia continued to feel the disappointment of her parents being gone most of the time. Instead of their company, she received expensive gifts. She had a whole room stuffed with all her toys. Her parents told her all the time how smart she was and told her she could be an attorney someday.

When Olivia was twelve years old, she won a talent show for her piano playing. She enjoyed band in school and continued to play competitively.

Her dad remained focused on his work as an attorney. He had a big case that year. To make sure the litigation was successful, he had to prepare almost nightly, month after month. He missed most of her recitals and performances.

When a dad isn't there for his little girl, she feels abandoned. She seeks to find her identity in other things, like excelling at school or boys (or both).

Olivia brought her emptiness and pain from her early childhood into her adolescent years. The combination of ambition and neglect created the perfect storm. Her hurt and anger continued to accumulate.

Olivia got into trouble occasionally. She picked on the girls who didn't dress as well as she could. She developed a reputation as a spoiled bully. Her parents didn't say much, so she didn't care. She couldn't tolerate school rules, and she didn't feel understood by anyone.

She felt superior to her classmates, many of whom looked up to her as the standard for how to dress. This attracted the wrong kind of attention. She attracted boys who had their own selfish desires in mind. Piano and grades were no longer first in her life.

I like having the attention on me. I feel good when others want to look like me.

Her dad wasn't at home much, so she looked elsewhere for male approval and attention. She started having sex at fourteen years old, which only resulted in further developing the wrong type of reputation at school. Her parents let her know they suspected she was too close to boys. They told her how such inappropriate behavior wasn't good for their family reputation. They reminded her that she should think about her future as an attorney. She would get angry and defensive, and she lied to them—denying any wrongdoing. Deep down she cared, but she never let them know this. Why should she be vulnerable if her parents didn't care about her feelings?

Chapter 10 — Olivia's Journey

Before she left for college, her dad made an attempt to connect with her by telling her she was growing up to be a beautiful young lady. Olivia couldn't accept the compliment. She felt his effort was too little, too late. He had lost her trust. On the outside, she agreed with her dad. *I look good.* But on the inside, she felt unlovable.

I'm good for my body and my piano playing, but nobody loves the real me. I'm not sure I know who the real me is. I'm unwanted. Dad only talks about me following in his footsteps. Mom is no better because she's focused on my piano playing. Why don't they ever try to understand what is really going on with me?

Olivia was overinvested in a negative image. Her worldview continued along its dim path. *Nobody cares about my suffering.* The darkness of Olivia's mind was enough to block out the image of her identity. Even when God pursued her through her parents, she couldn't accept their attempts at affirmation.

In college, she performed well at first, but when she started her core classes, she failed her first paralegal class. By then, she was more into partying and drugs than invested in learning. She continued her promiscuity.

Being clever, she was able to hide her immaturity. But soon her consistently poor grades caught up with her. Her parents realized their suspicions were true and pressed her for much-needed details. Finally, she admitted to partying instead of studying.

Yeah, I'm not happy. I'm living a lie. You don't care about me. Nobody does. Nobody knows who I am—I still don't know who I am.

With the details out in the open, her parents decided to bring her home. She dropped out of school and moved home. Within a week, she received a DUI. This forced her into a local recovery program. Her dad had connections that helped minimize her legal consequences. Fortunately, her parents had the resources to pay her legal fees and keep her in therapy.

Olivia, being insightful, responded to counseling. She started to realize all she had lost. She processed her childhood, learned what she missed, and learned how to receive from others who were capable of giving to her emotionally. However, God wasn't a part of her life. She still lived with strong, discouraging beliefs that caused her to focus on creation.

I'm done hooking up with guys. I'm ready to be married and start a family.

Olivia found a guy and started dating. She eventually married him but wasn't able to form a healthy relationship with her husband. She struggled to feel she was worth her husband's love. His focus on work and her temper didn't help matters.

One day, her husband came home from work and said he needed to talk to her. "I've been having an affair for two years. I ended it, and I want to work through this." He kept talking, but his words faded into the background as Olivia's chest pounded. Enraged, she lashed out at him, venting her anger until she finally collapsed on the couch in tears.

Rejected and alone again. I can't make it on my own. I'm not enough. I'm just a replaceable nobody. I can't handle being alone. I can't survive the humiliation. Something's deeply wrong with me. This is too much for me. I can't take this anymore.

Olivia worked on her marriage, but the recovery years were rough. She blew up in a jealous rage every time her husband shifted his attention away from her. The more she raged, the more he didn't want to be around her. The less interest he showed in her, the more insecure she felt and the angrier she became.

Olivia continued to feel lost. She accepted defeat and resigned to her negative self-image. She focused on her husband instead of feeling the pain of her own need. Deep down, she desired attention so she'd feel lovable.

Time passed. Olivia survived her marriage crisis and reconnected with her love of music.

I don't understand why I've been dealt such a difficult life. I'm glad the crisis is over. I'm thankful that when I play the piano I don't have to think about all the pain I've been through.

After Olivia repaired her marriage, she had two children. The next four years were average. She enjoyed raising her children, but her marriage was never the same. She decided to return to school to focus on a career in acting. She coped with her husband's empty words by focusing on her children and auditioning and participating in whatever work she could find.

Chapter 10 — Olivia's Journey

One day, Olivia's husband spoke words to her that signaled the end of the marriage: "I love you, but I'm not in love with you." Within a year, she was divorced and alone. Instead of grieving this loss, she pushed aside her feelings and redoubled her efforts to graduate from acting school.

If we could get inside her heart at this juncture to know what she wouldn't allow herself to feel, we'd hear this:

Life can be so unfair. Everything I've tried to avoid has happened anyway. I've been trying so hard for years. Will I ever find peace in life? There must be more to life. Nobody cares. I suffer for no reason. I'm unlovable. My situation is hopeless. I'm better off dead. I'm worthless. Why was I ever born? I'm not good at anything. Nothing is ever going to change.

After more months of loneliness, Olivia felt crushed to the point of desperation. Olivia returned to counseling and experienced some progress. Her counselor told her about the effects of abuse and neglect: "During your childhood, you received too much of what you didn't need. We call that abuse. And you didn't get enough of what you did need. We call that neglect. No wonder you gave up on school and relied on the boys and the men in your life."

I have to admit, deep down, I'm too focused on men. I don't need a man. I can take care of myself.

After Olivia graduated from acting school, she took side jobs while she waited for her big break. Craving attention, she continued to hook up with men to experience some closeness, but she never let herself feel her need for very long. She had some one-night stands and lived with various men for a few months at a time. Fed up with this routine, she kicked the last one out and refocused on her acting career.

Now she's finally caught a break and has become a regular on a soap opera. She continues to play the piano and spend time with her adult children.

I love entertaining people. I'm glad I decided to become an actress. My abuse and ex-husband are in the past. I enjoy playing piano when it doesn't remind me of my childhood struggles. My children follow my soap opera, which is sometimes scarily close to the life I lived.

Study Questions

1. What prevented Olivia from moving past her crisis?
2. Why didn't Olivia become a Christian?
3. Describe Olivia's self-image.
4. Can you relate to Olivia in any way? If so, how?
5. How is Olivia's journey the same or different than Andrew's and Samantha's?

Part III — God's Call

Chapter 11	**Identity Maturity**
Chapter 12	**Stage 1: Caregiver Focused**
Chapter 13	**Stage 2: Creation Focused**
Chapter 14	**Stage 3: Crisis Focused**
Chapter 15	**Stage 4: Christ Focused**
Chapter 16	**Stage 5: Calling Focused**
Chapter 17	**Going Beyond**

An inescapable reality and an intentional identity lead to an inevitable destiny. God has plans for you that only you can fulfill. Every day of your life has a clear purpose. God is working to make you complete.

>Jeremiah 29:11
Ephesians 2:10
Psalm 139:16
Psalm 138:8
Romans 8:29
1 Peter 5:10

Chapter 11

Identity Maturity

Identity maturity means your self-image (who you think you are) is moving toward your fixed identity (who God knows you to be). When you accept God and become a Christian, you gain access to your identity and are able to identify with Christ.

However, identification with Christ doesn't equal maturity in Christ. Going to church doesn't make you a Christian. When a student enrolls in college, she identifies with her major, but she isn't an expert. As she completes her assignments, she becomes more knowledgeable. Likewise, you start out knowing you belong to Christ, but you must work out what this means. With time, you become more mature and develop a deeper understanding of who you are—what it means to be you.

Life is a quest to discover who you are. You must go through the journey of becoming with all its bumps and bruises. Growth takes time and patience. Fulfilling your destiny is a developmental process. Your greatest joy comes as you know you're living the best life you can at any given moment.

When you read about the woman caught in adultery, have you ever wondered what happened to her after Jesus forgave her sins and told her to go in peace and sin no more (John 8:1–11)? I'm sure she was grateful Jesus didn't condemn her and have her stoned. The next day, though, she still had to work through her brokenness. *Why exactly was I sleeping with that man? What does this say about how I see myself and God?* Hopefully, she seized the opportunity to accept God's forgiveness and be free of sin.

God forgives you so you can move beyond your shameful experiences to purity and innocence. When the pain of staying the same is greater than the pain required to change, you become sufficiently motivated to grow. If you're blocking the pain, you're holding back your growth. However, if you're experiencing more pain than you can handle, you're too isolated from love.

When you accept God with a hungry, enthusiastic, and humble heart, you're on the path to identity maturity. To stay on the path and keep growing, you need to accept greater responsibility: make a serious effort to carry your own load. Just as importantly, you need to develop healthy relationships: connect with others so they can help carry your burdens, and you their burdens.

Recall from Chapter 1 that to grow toward your identity, you need balanced development in four life areas:
1. Social relationships (horizontal intimacy)
2. Skills to use in the world (ability, mastery, and achievements)
3. Self-awareness (understanding of your identity)
4. Spiritual connection to God (vertical intimacy)

No one can master all of these simultaneously. You'll need to work at each one throughout your lifetime. To become all God made you to be, you must focus on different goals at different times. It's important to develop an understanding of physical reality over the course of your life, but there's also a spiritual reality to discover and explore. When you become a Christian, you begin to strengthen your understanding of God and develop a worldview that furthers your understanding of creation and your identity.

At different times, you'll be able to make sense of life and enjoy it in different and deeper ways. Your childhood is different than your twenties; your twenties are different than your forties; your forties are different than your sixties, and so forth.

Young adulthood is a chance to experience the significant milestones of life like completing an education, starting a career, getting married, and having children. The investments you make during this stage help you can accomplish more later in life.

The second half of life mirrors the first half; you might call it your second childhood. You get a do-over, but this time you have half a lifetime's experience to guide you. You can apply all you've learned to make your signature contribution to the world. You can learn from your mistakes and fine-tune your legacy.

Eventually, your ability to give back will reach its peak. Your body will be depleted, but your spirit full of hope as you anticipate eternal glory (2 Corinthians 4:16–17).

Chapter 11 — Identity Maturity

Identity maturity requires both developmental and spiritual maturity. Physical birth starts you down the path of physical maturity, just as spiritual birth initiates growth in spiritual maturity. Some aspects of psychological development are prerequisites to spiritual growth. For example, a young child is limited to concrete thinking, only developing the capacity for abstract thought as he moves into adolescence.

A child can become a Christian, but since a child isn't fully developed and self-aware like an adult, a child can't know his identity as fully as an adult can. Later in life, a child gains self-awareness (usually during adolescence) and the potential to see the totality of his spiritual crisis. He can ask, *What is the meaning of life?* and more specifically, *What is the meaning of my life?*

Here are some of the other ways to describe this important developmental milestone:

- Puberty (developing a masculine or feminine identity)
- Abstract thinking (the ability to grasp ideas and concepts beyond the tangible)
- Self-awareness (being conscious of one's own thoughts, feelings, desires, and motives)
- Identity crisis (realization that self and/or purpose are insufficiently defined)
- Early adulthood (usually meaning someone who has recently finished adolescence)
- Responsible for self (gaining independence from a parent)
- The age of accountability (instead of relying on a parent's faith, a person can make her own decision)
- God becomes primary authority (parental authority is gradually transferred to God)
- Move beyond egocentrism (realization that others have different perspectives, experiences, and opinions—their own identity)

The spiritual crisis shouldn't be tied to a specific age. Some people delay facing the crisis by pushing it out into their twenties, thirties, and even beyond into a full-fledged midlife crisis. And as you'll see, some never make it there at all.

At the point of spiritual birth, you begin the three steps to loving God detailed in Chapter 7 (receiving, needing, and embracing God) as the solution to the crisis. This can happen in two ways: When spiritual birth comes before self-awareness, God can preserve and prepare the person for the crisis. When spiritual birth follows the crisis, it provides the much-needed solution.

The Path to Identity Maturity

We can divide life into two periods: before and after the point of spiritual crisis. Then, to further understand identity maturity, we can subdivide each period into a consuming (being and receiving) and producing (doing and giving) period. Now we can see identity maturing through five stages. I named each stage according to its primary developmental focus.

Stage 1: Caregiver Focused (immature consumer)
Stage 2: Creation Focused (immature producer)
Stage 3: Crisis Focused (transition and growth)
Stage 4: Christ Focused (mature consumer)
Stage 5: Calling Focused (mature producer)

The Five Stages of Identity Development

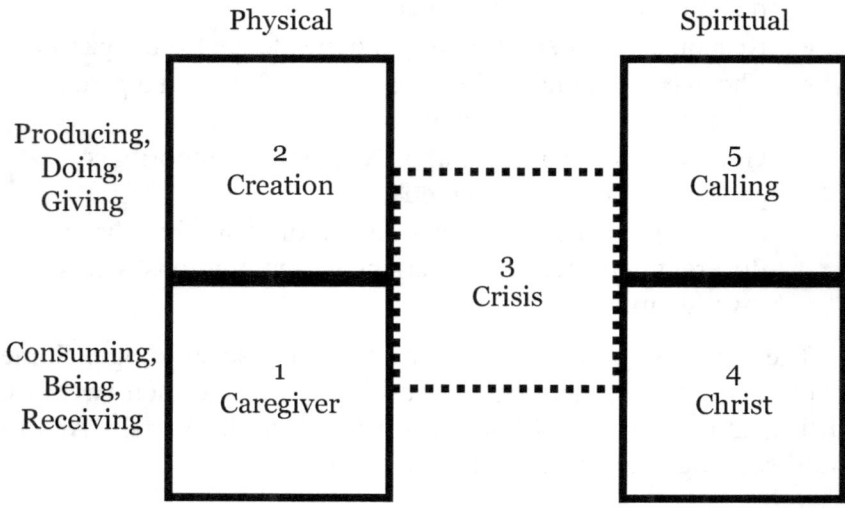

The stages have overlap, but each stage has a predominant focus. The stages are sequential, but the stage you're currently in doesn't have to be completely resolved before you can grow in the next stage. Throughout your life, you'll revisit the stages to complete what you didn't finish. You need growth opportunities (crises) to help you mature.

As the stages progress, you increase in awareness of your identity. Until you develop a spiritual awareness of God, even if you've fully mastered Stage 2 as a prolific producer, the moments of crisis in Stage 3 will be insurmountable—something to endure and escape, not to overcome. Conversely, a young follower of Christ will have a head start on Stage 4 but will still need to uncover the parts of his identity discoverable in earlier stages.

The first two stages focus on the concrete objectives, while the last two focus on spiritual objectives. To understand how to receive God (Stage 4), you need to have received love from caregivers (Stage 1). To understand how to serve God spiritually (Stage 5), you need to have learned how to be productive in creation (Stage 2). There's a crisis (Stage 3) in the middle of it all bridging the physical and spiritual realities and providing the catalyst for maturity.

As people mature, they progress through the five stages:

1. **Spiritually Immature Consumers are Caregiver Focused:** They focus inward to internalize a caregiver's love and learn that the world is a place where needs are met. Immature consumers lack an awareness of their identity, so they can't effectively contribute. Such people consume only for self and might believe life should dazzle and entertain. *I shouldn't have to work too hard. Life should be fun and easy. My needs should be promptly met in full by others. I feel good only when I receive from others.*
2. **Spiritually Immature Producers are Creation Focused:** They focus outward to externalize abilities and learn about the world (creation). Such people produce almost exclusively for their own benefit. *I have value only when I produce. I love the way I feel when other people appreciate my contributions. I enjoy cooking food, fixing cars, and coaching soccer.*
3. **Physically Mature Discontented People are Crisis Focused:** They focus on the crisis because they can't find satisfaction with

creation or God. They can find superficial contentment, but it lasts only a short time and has no associated meaning. If spiritual birth hasn't occurred yet, they will focus on life experiences. Non-Christians won't be able to progress beyond this level. Instead, the best they can do is remain stuck, perpetually trying to find meaning and purpose for their existence. At worst, they will remain creation or caregiver focused. Meaning will be derived from creation. But once spiritual birth occurs, an alternative path opens, providing the ability to see beyond creation to God's spiritual realm. *There are problems I don't have the power or cleverness to fix. And when I try to cope, I make myself sick and poor with all the things I consume. I'm letting down the people who depend on me. I wish I felt some purpose to my life.*

4. **Spiritually Mature Consumers are Christ Focused:** They focus inward to develop a worldview and identity that result in meaning and purpose. Meaning is derived from the Creator. *I consume to meet my own needs but also to receive the strength and skills I'll need to be able to meet the needs of others. My Christian community is a place where I receive from others so I can mature into all God made me to be.*

5. **Spiritually Mature Producers are Calling Focused:** They focus outward, producing spiritual fruit to show Christ to the world. Christians have something significant to contribute to the world. *I recognize the need to give to others, I can give without expecting something in return. I've received enough from God, and now I have the desire and resources to advance God's kingdom.*

People need both a consumer and a producer focus. Even a mature adult needs to receive from others some of the time. A mature adult can accept that life will sometimes be a challenging struggle that includes suffering.

The younger you are, the more you'll be a consumer by default. Being a consumer isn't bad. As a consumer, you receive what you need from others. You're only selfish when you're wasteful and indulgent at the expense of others. Even a five-year-old can produce or give back something. But a five-year-old will be a consumer most of the time.

Receiving prepares you for giving. You need to receive until you have enough to give. If you've received enough in the first part of life, you'll be prepared to give generously in a healthy way during the second part. The goal is to reach a tipping point where you are full enough that you can contribute into others' lives from a place of emotional stability.

The older you are, the more you should develop the capacity to produce. This doesn't mean your sole purpose in life is to be a vending machine that meets others' needs. Being a producer is personal and relational. There is joy in producing when you contribute according to the identity God gave you.

If you find yourself producing without joy, you might be burned out. You become depleted when you receive insufficient care or you use yourself beyond the capacity God has in mind for you. You can make corrections with some combination of
1. receiving (internalizing that you're loved and accepted),
2. growing (expanding the capacity of your self-image),
3. reducing your workload to fit within your capacity, and
4. increasing your capacity for suffering (doing without).

You'll thrive only when you keep yourself within the limits of God's intentions. Whenever Jesus ministered to others to the point of exhaustion, He then needed to spend some time alone with the Father. If you feel stretched and exhausted some days, that's probably healthy. Stretching is good, but unrelenting depletion, panic, or despair are bad.

Our response to life can be healthy (growing and moving forward) or unhealthy (stagnating in a stage or regressing to a previous stage). If we also consider our success or failure in navigating our spiritual crisis, this gives us four ways to measure identity maturity:
1. A **healthy Christian** will reach the crisis stage and resolve it by seeing God as the answer to the meaning of life. He moves on to become Christ focused, then calling focused as he seeks to further God's kingdom, before he enters into heaven.

2. An **unhealthy Christian** has experienced spiritual rebirth; however, she struggles to untangle herself from the world and sin. Her flesh dominates her life. Her understanding is confused by worldly wisdom, so she never fully resolves the spiritual crisis. She is saved and will make it to heaven but won't bear much fruit in the meantime.
3. A **healthy non-Christian** accomplishes all the earthly developmental tasks but lacks spiritual understanding. She will never quite grasp the true meaning of life. Though a highly productive member of society, she won't be able to enter heaven.
4. An **unhealthy non-Christian** fails to mature in both the earthly developmental sense and the heavenly spiritual sense. He remains a drain on society and won't be able to enter heaven.

The following diagram illustrates common scenarios of how a person can pass through (solid line) or reside within (dashed line) the five stages.

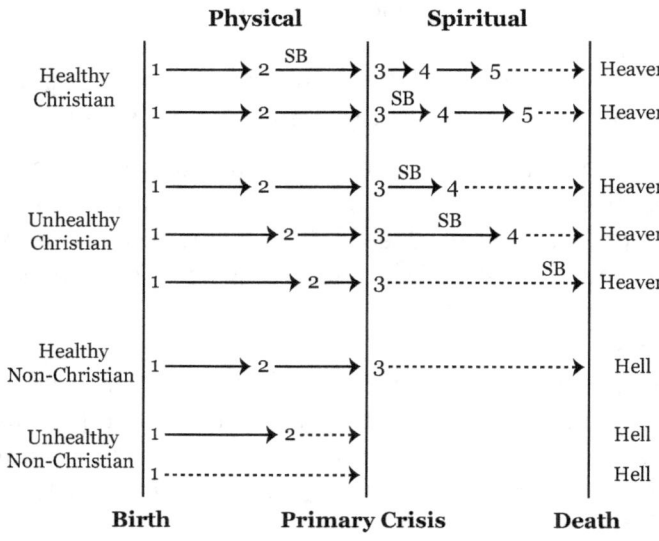

1=Caregiver, 2=Creation, 3=Crisis, 4=Christ, 5=Calling; SB=Spiritual Birth

Let's revisit Andrew's, Samantha's, and Olivia's stories to see how they navigate the five stages of identity maturity. A fourth example of an unhealthy non-Christian is unnecessary. He'd be like

Andrew before he moved past his crisis and like Olivia in her struggle to see God.

Andrew as a Healthy Christian

Andrew struggles at first to move beyond even the first stage of being caregiver focused, but his encounters with reality and becoming a Christian help him mature into the final calling-focused stage.

When Andrew manages to finally transition out of the caregiver-focused stage, he has a lot of growth ahead of him. He knows he is supposed to receive from God and serve others, but he doesn't quite know how. He hasn't developed much of a sense of identity, let alone tested it in the midst of crisis. Instead of following a linear progression through the five stages, Andrew will need to shift his focus between creation (learning how to provide for others), crisis (learning to rely on God), and Christ (learning to find meaning in God). As he perseveres, God will help him correct his self-image from "hopeless dependent" to "son of God" to "significant contributor." Andrew then moves into the fifth and final stage, calling focused, and acts in God's power to advance His kingdom.

Samantha as an Unhealthy Christian

Samantha becomes a Christian, but can't overcome her past, move beyond her crisis, and become calling focused.

Samantha didn't receive what she needed during the caregiver-focused stage of her life, and this neglect has taught her to rely on creation and her own resourcefulness. Instead of trusting God to guide her through her times of crisis, she blames Him for allowing the suffering to occur. She's stuck bouncing back and forth between creation and crisis focused. While she occasionally tries to be Christ focused, her efforts are short-lived. She trusts God for salvation but remains immature in Christ.

To move forward, she firsts need to take an honest look at the neglect in her past and let God heal those emotional injuries. Then she must accept that her true identity comes from God, not from the nature of her circumstances. Otherwise, at the next moment of crisis, she will once again feel betrayed and abandoned by God.

Olivia as a Healthy Non-Christian

Olivia is creation focused and struggles to find success and fulfillment within that stage. She fails to see God during the crisis points in her life, so she refocuses on creation and looks for comfort there.

Olivia received the basic attention and affirmation she needed as a child during the caregiver-focused stage. And she has learned how to interact with creation in healthy, nondestructive ways. But her times of crisis have not led her to God. She has developed ways of enduring pain, insecurity, and unfulfillment. Instead of looking for deeper satisfaction, meaning, or purpose, she is resigned to the unhappiness that lies beneath the surface of her comfortable life.

Roadblocks to Identity Maturity

Life is tough. Because of evil, sin, and brokenness, anyone can become stuck at any stage in many different ways. However, no matter where or how they're stuck, they have the same problem of a misplaced identity.

An identity crisis is truly a spiritual crisis. You'll never understand who you really are until you look beyond creation to your Creator.

A person who becomes stuck in one of the first three stages is likely struggling with a personality weakness. She doesn't derive her sense of worth from a relationship with God or a recognition that He specially designed her identity. Her crisis can't be resolved by creation because creation can't define who she is. To reach the final two stages and become a confident Christian, she needs to look at who she is, not at what's available to her in creation.

Chapter 11 — Identity Maturity

The following table describes various people stuck in their immaturity. All of these people base their self-worth on a false premise. They take on a caricature to avoid their painful reality, giving up the opportunity to be who God made them to be.

Caricature	Self-Worth	Avoids	Stage
The Passive Dependent	Being cared for	Struggle to grow and accept responsibility	1
The Aggressive Counter-Dependent	Putting others down	Disappointment from relationships	1
The Thrill-Seeking Addict	Feeling pleasure	Pain from perceived inadequacy	2
The Skin-Deep Attention-Seeker	Attracting interest	Overcoming insecurities	2
The Context Controller	Experiencing all is right in the world	Facing the reality of suffering	2
The Perfectionistic Producer	Accomplishing tasks	Awareness of weaknesses	2
The Preoccupied Codependent/Enabler	Fulfilling a role; value to others	Becoming in touch with own preferences	2
The Blinded Radical	Recreating self in own image	God's absolute design	3
The Isolating Independent	Self-sufficiency	Intimacy	3

The next five chapters will reference the caricatures. Each chapter explores a stage and provides details on how to become unstuck.

Study Questions

1. Which stage of identity development are you in currently?
2. How balanced is your pursuit of the four life areas (Social, Skills, Self-awareness, Spiritual)?
3. What prevented Samantha from connecting more with God and becoming Calling focused, able to do more with her life?
4. Was there a turning point in Samantha's life? If so, why did she fail to take full advantage of it?
5. Was there a turning point in Olivia's life? If so, why did she fail to take full advantage of it?
6. Which caricature, or false self-image, from the chart above is most familiar to you?
7. What appears to be holding you back from developing a mature identity?
8. What do you think it will take for you to reach the final calling-focused stage?

Chapter 12

Stage 1: Caregiver Focused

A caregiver provides care and love. A dependent attaches to the caregiver and receives love. A person with a caregiver-focused identity allows a select person to meet most of his needs and wants. When this arrangement is healthy, the caregiver provides what the dependent needs without hindering the natural growth process.

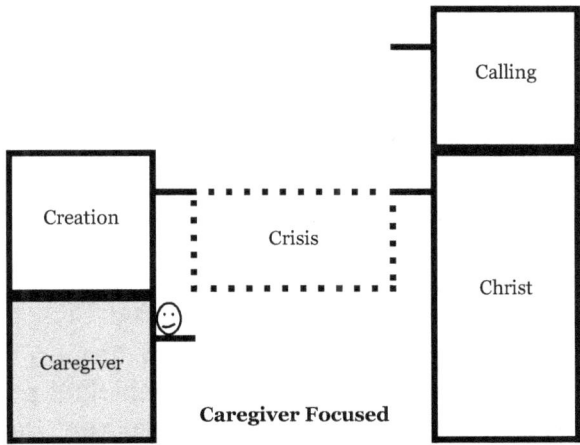

Healthy dependence ensures you get what you need from others. Healthy dependence prepares the way for independence, while unhealthy dependence blocks the path to independence.

Dependence is normal and healthy no matter how old you are. Everyone relies on others for many aspects of daily life. However, the amount you rely on others should track with norms and shift considerably over your lifetime. The dependence chart (see following page) illustrates a healthy person's change in dependence over time.

As a child, you depended on others for most things in life. Your self-image was mostly undefined and unexplored. You consumed what others produced. Your ability to produce and carry your own weight was severely limited.

TO IDENTITY AND BEYOND

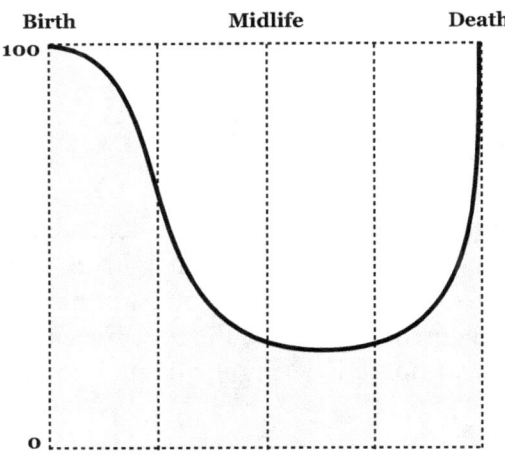

Dependence From Birth to Death

Physically, you couldn't do many things for yourself. You relied on others to do things for you, like make your food, dress you, or even help you go to the bathroom. Emotionally, you were tied to the one who cared for you. But that tie is no longer appropriate. As long as you exist as an extension of your caregiver, you won't be able to develop your own identity.

On one level, everyone is dependent. Even the most independent person must rely on God. Dependence is an integral part of God's plan. Only God is completely independent, so you'll always need Him. God designed you to need others for emotional fulfillment and assistance with complicated tasks. But in many cases, dependence is meant to be temporary.

You're designed to grow in your identity and move to the next stage. A dependent baby is cute. But a dependent (immature) adult is draining. A healthy person accepts the challenge to grow and takes on tasks suitable to his abilities. When you were a baby, you depended on your mother to dress you; now that you're older, you dress yourself.

Recognize an Unhealthy Focus

The movie *Groundhog Day* is about Phil, a self-centered, entitled weatherman who matures into an independent guy. The more immature he acts (by seeking his pleasure at the expense of others), the more he repels others. The more confident he becomes (by developing his own identity), the more he attracts others. Phil isn't necessarily a Christian, but the movie illustrates what it's like to mature emotionally.

Unhealthy dependence means you allow others to do for you what you should be doing yourself. If you allow this interference, your growth will be stunted, and you'll fall short of your God-given identity. A lack of identity will both cause others to miss out on who you are as a complete minister of God's grace and prevent you from enjoying yourself at the depth God intended.

Other people depend on the fruit you produce when you exercise the spiritual gifts God gave you. Maybe you're a genius with numbers. Maybe your words provide much needed clarity and direction. Maybe your encouragement is life giving. Your essential contribution to God's kingdom won't be realized if you're stuck being caregiver focused.

God is a social being. Since you're made in God's image, you're a social being too. The core of who you are is oriented toward relating to others. Even the least social person must rely on others often. The chief obstacle to maturity isn't dependence—it's a lack of the sort of support that promotes independence.

Following are two examples of dependent behavior.

The Passive Dependent

As a passive dependent, your primary worth is based upon receiving care from others. You're more likely to avoid God. You avoid the struggle to grow and accept responsibility. If you're married, you're likely too close to family and not close enough to your spouse; you've failed to leave and cleave.

A dependent person usually has a partner-in-crime, a codependent who enables his immaturity. A father spoils his child. A wife sets aside her identity in order to make her husband look good all the time. The dependent person ends up developing a sense of entitlement. *I should get what I want whenever I want it.* He's able to accept care but merely consumes it instead of harnessing it toward his own self-growth. He perpetually needs more. Andrew is a good example of this type of person (see Chapter 8).

The story of the prodigal son (Luke 15) illustrates a person who started out dependent but successfully graduated to independent. The prodigal son asked his father for his inheritance so he could live the easy life. He was immature, irresponsible, and wanted instant gratification. He had the emotional maturity of a teenager, and perhaps that's how old he was. He lacked self-worth and any significant skills that would have allowed him to contribute to the benefit of others. But when his money ran out, he didn't go begging for more. Instead, he was willing to take an unskilled job. He accepted responsibility for himself. Lesson learned.

As a dependent, you're missing the knowledge that you have the potential to contribute to others, resulting in a lack of maturity, purpose, and identity. You might have thoughts like these:

I have needs; therefore, they should be met.

I deserve whatever I can get from others to make my life easier.

Avoiding others is easier than knowing myself and making myself known.

The Aggressive Dependent

An aggressive dependent, or counter-dependent, is also immature. A counter-dependent projects toughness on the outside, but remains fragile on the inside. For example, a bully appears to be invincible until confronted, and then she backs down quickly, revealing extreme neediness.

The movie *The Bridge to Terabithia* contains several examples of counter-dependency. Janice Avery, a large eight-grader, blocks the entrances to the bathrooms at recess, requiring each "customer" to pay her a dollar. Later on, after a trick is played on her, she caves in emotionally and we find out she has an abusive father. After she experiences her own humiliation, she chooses to defend her classmates against other bullies.

An aggressive dependent attempts to control her life by moving against others in the name of self-preservation. To eliminate the risk of not having her needs met, she demands that others give to her. Olivia exemplified this type of person when she made fun of her peers' inability to dress with style (see Chapter 10). But she still needed her parents to take care of her into her twenties.

If you're counter-dependent, you're capable of standing up for yourself, and you expect others to act according to your wishes. You use power to alienate others so you'll feel safe. You try to exercise authority without first working to earn that privilege. You can blame and attack others, pointing the finger at others without looking at your own weakness. To avoid the pain of admitting weakness, you try to dominate others.

You might have thoughts like these:

It is your fault we don't have a better relationship.

Others can't or won't come through for me, so I have to take charge and make it happen.

I feel better when everything goes my way.

Plan to Be Creation Focused

To move beyond an unhealthy caregiver focus, try the following strategies.

Check If You're Stuck Focusing on Caregivers

If you're stuck, you've probably formed an unhealthy symbiotic relationship with an important caregiver in your life. If your caregiver's primary source of her identity comes from over-functioning in your life, she might be better called a care*taker* or enabler.

Is your sense of well-being based on how well others take care of you? Are you unable or unwilling to invest in contributing to others? Do you ignore opportunities to discover your identity?

If so, you have only the beginnings of a developed identity. Until your identity matures, you'll continue to borrow the identity of your caregiver. See if any of these descriptions ring true:

- You lack any specific, realistic life plans.
- You're directionless or jobless.
- You're fixated on one person who seems able to meet all your needs.

- You struggle to make sense of life or make it work the way you want.
- You don't have specific desires for how you want to make a living or spend your time.
- You're still living with, or financially dependent upon, your parents in your late-twenties and beyond.

Implement Solutions for Becoming Unstuck

God calls all of us to participate in the work necessary to mature. To become unstuck, consider which of the following actions are appropriate for your situation and then carry them out:

- Seek nurturing from healthy adults who also can set clear limits on their time.
- Accept yourself no matter where you're at in your journey. Practice *being* before *doing*.
- Accept what others have to offer and move forward with your life.
- Practice being independent by trying to do things yourself.
- Ask for help only if you really need it.
- Refuse help when it interferes with an opportunity to struggle and grow through a problem.
- Make a list of new things to experience (hobbies, jobs, relationships, etc.). Try them all and evaluate your experience.
- Be financially responsible. Get and keep a job. Pay for all of your expenses.

Check If You're Ready to Be Creation Focused

As a healthy person, you'll continue to need support from your caregivers, but the nature of the support you require has changed. You need assistance, but not too much or too little of it. Make sure your caregivers are promoting independence, not enabling weakness:

- They should be more interested in listening and encouraging than offering to fix your problems for you.
- They should help you talk through situations without telling you exactly what to do.

- They should tell you the truth instead of what you want to hear.
- They should offer you fellowship, not lodging.

You're ready to be creation focused when you have
- a positive view of others: *I have access to help when I need it;* and
- a positive view of self: *I'm valued for who I am, and I can accomplish some activities without help.*

Also check to make sure you
- have internalized a sense of love from primary caregivers,
- are secure in being (self-acceptance) without doing (deriving worth from performance),
- are curious about exploring the external world,
- desire to build competency, and
- want to develop responsibility and make contributions.

An adult who matures beyond the caregiver stage becomes independent and eventually interdependent. He depends on others for some things he could do himself, if only he weren't so busy. The overall amount of work balances out according to each person's ability. For example, a wife might work only inside the home while her husband earns all the money they need. The wife could work outside the home, but she depends on her husband financially. The husband could perform many of the daily household tasks, but he depends on his wife.

Everyone needs to feel cared for. It's a normal part of life. But refusing to grow up according to your God-given ability is too much dependence. It's unhealthy for both the caregiver and the dependent. Learning responsibility is usually an uncomfortable emotional experience at first. However, as we'll see in the next chapter, the benefits far outweigh way the discomfort.

You never stop needing others, but you do become increasingly independent, and then interdependent, as you become who God made you to be.

Study Questions

1. In what ways can you identify with passive dependence?
2. In what ways can you identify with aggressive dependence?
3. Make a list of at least ten ways you're dependent on others.
   - How would your life be different if you could no longer depend on others in these areas?
   - How many of these could you do yourself if you had to? In what areas are you truly and fully reliant on others?
   - If you've discovered you're too dependent or too counter-dependent, how can you become more balanced?

Chapter 13

Stage 2: Creation Focused

Creation includes everything in existence except God. God made us with both an internal and an external world to explore. However, during Stage 2 of identity development, you base your identity on external activities. Focusing on the external allows you to update your self-image based on what you discover about your abilities. To get to know yourself, you have to experience yourself interacting with creation.

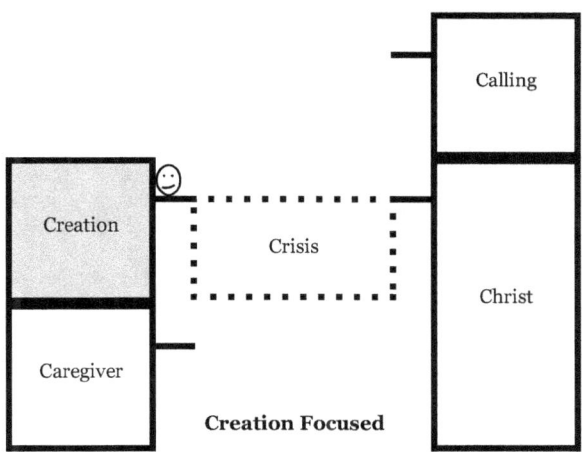

Creation Focused

You grow by exploring which "external somethings," beyond your caregiver, will help you discover who you are. You learn what you're good at and what you're not so good at. Which of your skills are above average? A parent can usually tell at an early age which of their child's abilities are exceptional.

God designed you so that you won't be able to reach your potential on your own. You must add an outside factor to maximize your potential and your life satisfaction. The thing you choose to add makes all the difference.

You + ? = Maximum Potential and Satisfaction

Creation offers many possible additives. From Chapter 2, recall the list of people and things you can look to in order to acquire an identity. You might rely on your performance or the effects of a drug as the source of your satisfaction. You've already learned that looking to creation for identity is like putting on a costume. It's an act that falls short of God's intentions.

You can't maximize potential and satisfaction by pretending to be someone you're not. At best, *you* plus *creation* results in earthly achievements. At worst, the combination produces shame and addiction.

You + *Right Use of Creation* = Earthly Achievements
You + *Wrong Use of Creation* = Shame and Addiction

But how can we improve upon the right use of creation? We all start out accepting a caregiver as our vital missing piece. The goal is to transition first to creation, then to the Creator. Many things fulfill in part, but *God* provides deeper and more lasting fulfillment than earthly achievements.

God's offers us this spiritual formula:

Branches + *Vine* = Fruit
You + *Jesus* = Kingdom Achievement

"I am the vine; you are the branches.
Whoever abides in me and I in him,
he it is that bears much fruit,
for apart from me you can do nothing."
—John 15:5

Recognize an Unhealthy Focus

When you lean too heavily on something external other than God to define your identity, you're missing out on God's best for you. God intends for you to focus externally, but it also comes with the risk of ultimately worshipping creation rather than the Creator (Matthew 6:24). You can measure your dysfunction by how much

Chapter 13 — Stage 2: Creation Focused

you lose the sense of who you are when you lose what you've been relying on (for example, a job).

The external something can become a distracting decoy. The distraction keeps your focus off of God as well as any uncomfortable circumstances. This might sound like an acceptable tradeoff, but avoiding pain encourages infection, not healing.

The story of the prodigal son (Luke 15) illustrates how a hopelessly unhealthy focus on creation can become healthy. The prodigal son starts out a seeker of superficial pleasures: he consumes his father's wealth, living only for the moment. When he hits rock bottom, he realizes his sin. He desires to contribute and not merely consume. He returns better for the wear. Humbled, he is ready to work for his father.

> *"Not long after that, the younger son got together all he had, set off for a distant country and there squandered his wealth in wild living. After he had spent everything, there was a severe famine in that whole country, and he began to be in need. So he went and hired himself out to a citizen of that country, who sent him to his fields to feed pigs. He longed to fill his stomach with the pods that the pigs were eating, but no one gave him anything."*
> —Luke 15:13–16

You might think that the prodigal son's older brother is a mature producer because he works so hard for his father, but he is more of an immature producer. He struggles with self-righteousness and is unaware of how he too falls short. He is reluctant to give up his good image for something deeper and lasting. The older, conforming brother avoids seeking after his true identity.

> *"The older brother became angry and refused to go in. So his father went out and pleaded with him. But he answered his father, 'Look! All these years I've been slaving for you and never*

> *disobeyed your orders. Yet you never gave me even a young goat so I could celebrate with my friends. But when this son of yours who has squandered your property with prostitutes comes home, you kill the fattened calf for him!'"*
> —Luke 15:28–30

A child's self-image, without intentional parenting based on the Bible, can become bound to worldly values instead of God's intentional design. What follows then is identity confusion. For example, you may wonder: *Am I valuable only if I'm able to make a lot of money?*

Mastering how to interact with creation is a necessary focus on your way to becoming a mature producer. In childhood, a person learns how to ride a bike, work math problems, write sentences, complete household chores, play games and sports, and develop friendships. If she becomes fixated on superficial achievements or rewards while neglecting the internal and spiritual, she'll slow or sabotage identity development. Your *primary* sense of self-worth shouldn't come from earthly accomplishments.

When a child first learns to ride his bike, he might say, *Look at me, Mom. Look what I can do!* The child's caregiver needs are being met when his mom responds enthusiastically with *Look at you. You can ride your bike! I'm so proud of you.*

This is good as long as the child doesn't learn that his identity is tied to his performance. If mom criticizes the child's identity—*You're still not doing it right. You'll never amount to anything. Why can't you be more like your sister?*—the child will feel shame and could become fixated on performing to meet emotional needs. Such a situation is ripe for an addiction.

Addiction is more than selfishness—to be addicted, you must also be deceived. You think you're happy when you're really not. You have an unhealthy reliance on creation. Your sense of well-being is dependent on something other than your identity or God. Creation is good and can help you understand elements of who you are, but it only goes so far. For a complete identity, you need God.

Life presents many opportunities for short-term fulfillment—a shortcut to happiness that avoids suffering. These shortcuts always involve using creation in ways God never intended. By misusing creation, you ignore the reality God has created. You may acknowledge that God is real, but He seems distant and unreachable. So you become numb to God. You're better off working to understand how to use creation as God intends.

You know you're addicted when you continue to try to enjoy something beyond its intended capacity to produce enjoyment.

Addiction can occur when you engage in a superficially satisfying activity while mired in unpleasant feelings of emptiness. You're vulnerable when you're often feeling anxious, insecure, undefined, lost, rejected, forgotten, unimportant, insignificant, unwanted, or cast aside. Who wouldn't want relief from feelings like these?

When you're addicted, your ability to feel pleasantly satisfied is malfunctioning. To experience contentment and break addiction's hold on you, you must learn to be satisfied with less: that which previously hasn't been enough. This might sound like a no-win situation. Eating vegetables, for example, can sound like an awful idea when you're fixated on cake. However, once you experience how much your body prefers vegetables, you'll see the win. Only then can you move on to further growth.

Intermittent reward is enough to keep anyone eating. Once you associate a positive feeling with your behavior, a logical conclusion is "more is better." When you stop feeling good after you eat a delicious meal, you'll want to eat another meal in order to feel good again. But you have a problem of diminishing returns. There is a direct relationship between how quickly you feel good and how quickly that feeling will wear off. The faster the good feeling arrives, the emptier you'll feel when the feeling leaves.

Candy never completely fulfills your hunger, but it produces a pleasant feeling most of the time. You can become hooked on the short-term effects as long as there is some promise of reward. Candy tastes great but doesn't provide much lasting nourishment. And if you try to eat ten candy bars in a day, you're not going to feel much better (actually, you'll probably feel worse) than if you'd only eaten one. As you overwhelm your senses, you diminish the value of a good thing. Too much of a good thing isn't good.

Once addicted, you might be tempted to try to "fake it until you make it." This becomes a real problem if your efforts while faking it never allow you to make it. You'll be stuck faking it when the goal is to grow up and move on to the next stage.

Following are five examples of people caught up in the wrong use of God's creation. They illustrate what happens when *you*-plus-*something* goes bad. As you read about them, notice their similarities and their differences. It's no accident that people choose an external focus related to their strengths. But a strength used the wrong way is a weakness. The external focus on producing an exceptional outcome compensates for internal emptiness or chaos. This dichotomy results in addiction, idolatry, and loss of authenticity. Notice how all five misplace their identity when they prioritize immediate fulfillment.

The Thrill-Seeking Addict

The addict is hindered by his very senses, which he overloads to relieve the pain he feels. The thrill-seeker overinvests in pleasure, seeking to cover up the pain of inadequacy, the negative feelings of falling short. This makes it all too easy to base his primary worth upon his ability to escape reality by creating a fantasy (unreality) where he always feels good. As he focuses on making pleasure and pain relief his primary goal, he risks regressing back to an irresponsible dependent. Andrew showed this trait when he became immersed in his game worlds (see Chapter 8).

The Skin-Deep Attention Seeker

The attention seeker's primary worth is based upon the attention she receives because of her physical appearance. She avoids the struggle to grow and overcome her insecurities. She compares herself to others too much. By focusing on her outward appearance, she neglects an inner transformation. Often she will use her external beauty (God's gift to her) as a way to compensate for undeveloped internal beauty. Olivia acted this way when she emphasized her style of dress as better than others (see Chapter 10).

The Context Controller

The controlling person's appreciation of order becomes a weakness when she attempts to use order to eliminate the harshness of life. Her primary worth is based upon experiencing that *all* is right in the world. She avoids facing the reality of suffering. *I shouldn't have to suffer.* Her purpose in life is to build a perfect, pain-free environment. She attempts to make the world into a paradise—but this isn't God's goal. God wants us to be like Christ in an imperfect world, not to make an imperfect world perfect. Samantha demonstrated this unhealthy pursuit of control when she habitually purged her food (see Chapter 9).

The Perfectionistic Producer

A classic strength, using intelligence to solve problems, becomes a weakness when the passion for achievement consumes a person's sense of identity. The perfectionist tries not to acknowledge his vulnerability and weaknesses. But instead of seeking pleasure like the thrill-seeker, he seeks to boost his primary worth through accomplishments. He might love his job too much. He might love money too much. He will feel good about himself as long as he is attaining some external achievement. The prodigal son's older brother is a good example of this kind of person because he worked hard for his father without connecting with him.

The Codependent Enabler

Compassion and sensitivity to other people's pain become a weakness when this external focus takes priority over self-care and self-respect. The enabler's primary worth is based upon fulfilling her role. She desires to maintain her usefulness in relationship. She avoids getting in touch with her own longings and preferences. Her desire to be married could cause such an imbalance. She could take care of her spouse or her children too much, such that they never have to face their own limitations. Andrew's mom demonstrates this type of enabling when she over-functions in Andrew's life (see Chapter 8).

Plan to Be Crisis Focused

To move beyond an unhealthy creation focus, try the following.

Check If You're Stuck Focusing on Creation

If you wonder if you've become fixated on creation instead of your Creator, see if any of this sounds familiar:
- Your earthly focus dominates your life.
- You rely on creation to maintain a positive mood (addictive behaviors).
- You're mesmerized only by what is immediately in front of you (the next high).
- You have a consistent desire to escape or avoid reality.
- You're incapable of facing life's difficulties, so you're not growing.
- You don't feel your need for God.

Implement Solutions for Becoming Unstuck

To change your focus, you'll need to change your lifestyle. Otherwise you'll quickly be back consuming and chasing the same old things. Permanent solutions truly quench a person's thirst. But they require faith and patience. Maturing requires a high degree of investment. Growth allows for deeper fulfillment. When you stretch yourself, you increase your potential. This strain increases discomfort but also produces more desire. After you live up to your potential in a new way, you're ready for another stretch. The excitement of healthy growth is often the antidote to the boredom and superficiality of an unhealthy, addicted life.

To become unstuck, consider which of the following strategies are appropriate for your situation and carry them out:
- Variety and balance are good. Some escape is healthy. Include both fun activities and planned times for growth. Temporarily escaping the harshness of life and eliminating self-defeating thoughts are blessings.

- Avoid relying exclusively on any one particular person or aspect of creation. Stop expecting creation to fulfill your deepest longings. Don't be surprised when life disappoints you.
- Spend time learning God's intentions for creation. When you expect from creation what God intended, you'll also experience the joy God intended.
- Learn contentment. Reprioritize your desires (see Chapter 5).

Check If You're Ready to Be Crisis Focused

As a healthy person, you should find joy in productivity in at least one of the following areas:
- Academic or intellectual
- Athletic
- Artistic
- Social or relational
- Other healthy play and interaction with creation

You'll know you're ready to be crisis focused when you have
- the ability to enjoy life: *I excel at some part of life and I have something to contribute;* and
- a positive respect for the challenges of life: *There's a lot I don't understand about life.*

These are some more indicators that you're ready to move on to the next stage:
- You realize that money can't buy happiness.
- You recognize that something is horribly wrong with life.
- You feel empty—you've reached the bottom.
- You crave something beyond the immediate pleasures of creation.
- You're curious about finding meaning in life.

The only way to stop relying on creation to satisfy you is to experience a spiritual renewal. To be ready for renewal, you need to reach bottom (face your emptiness) by experiencing the crisis that creation can't fill your deepest longings. You must empty yourself of this hope so you can receive from God instead.

This isn't fulfilling. The good feeling doesn't last. There's got to be more.

There is a time to allow your desires to be filled and a time to wait patiently. Invest in the time it takes to develop your identity. The payoff is both immediate and eternal.

A crisis demonstrates that nothing in creation is able to give you meaning and purpose. So instead you look inward, where God is waiting as your source of fulfillment. Your crisis may or may not cause you to suffer, but it will stoke your curiosity. You will long to understand the meaning and purpose of your life.

Chapter 13 — Stage 2: Creation Focused

Study Questions

1. Are you more committed to instant gratification or delayed gratification?
2. Using something beyond God's intentions won't produce lasting happiness or joy. Do you have unrealistic expectations about the fulfillment you might receive from some aspects of creation (such as your spouse, career, food, etc.)?
3. Which of your strengths have become a weakness, a real liability?
4. What elements of creation do you struggle to use in the way God intended? Are you most like the thrill-seeker, the attention-seeker, the controller, the perfectionist, or the enabler?
5. What causes you the most shame?

Chapter 14

Stage 3: Crisis Focused

A crisis is the gap between the physical and the spiritual realities. God's grace bridges the gap, and faith allows passage over the spiritual bridge. If you never experienced a crisis, you'd never feel your need for God. Difficult moments should prompt you to activate your faith; until you do so, you'll be stuck within the crisis.

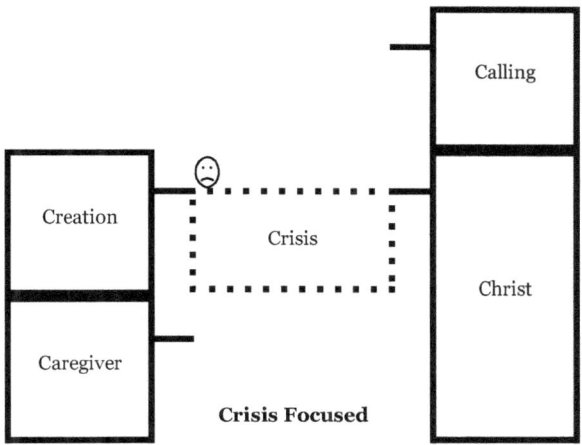

A crisis-focused person is plagued with doubt and feels trapped. He's in crisis mode. On the one hand, he has tasted that creation doesn't completely satisfy. On the other hand, he distrusts God. He's stuck between a rock and a hard place. His worldview can't explain his life experiences. He has no answer to why people suffer. Without God, he can only look to creation for answers.

Does anyone care? Will creation satisfy my needs?

Does God care? Did God just betray me? Can God satisfy my needs?

In searching for his identity, he might look to creation to find his identity, find initial success, and become complacent. But creation will eventually disappoint him, and he'll be faced with the crisis again.

Crisis Focused

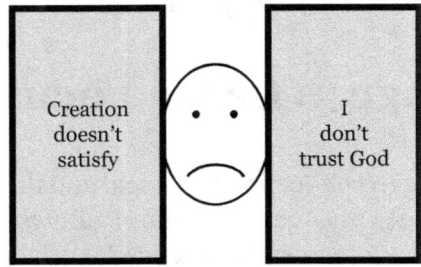

Stuck between two unpleasant realities

If a man looks for his identity in his job and he loses it, this will throw him into a crisis. *I lost my job. I don't know how I'm going to provide for myself. I don't know who I am. I'll get drunk.*

He makes an unhealthy choice to avoid feeling the shame of losing his identity. He hasn't really lost his identity, but he feels that way because his self-image is tied to his job.

A crisis ultimately challenges your connection to God. If your connection is weak, you'll want to focus on creation. A Christian can be in crisis without being crisis focused. She trusts God and works to bring her worldview into alignment with God's reality.

To graduate from being creation focused, you must realize that creation alone isn't enough to satisfy your deepest longings. If you can no longer make yourself happy by consuming whatever you want, what will you do instead? Having concluded that attempts at superficial fulfillment fall short, you'll develop a readiness to invest in a solution that lasts long-term.

You must strip away all that prevents you from feeling discontent. With the external distractions gone, you'll reach a point of crisis because you'll realize that you don't know enough of who you are. Racked with an undeniable feeling of emptiness, you'll finally be willing to look at life differently and develop a more sophisticated worldview.

You have to honestly conclude that the things of life have not and cannot fulfill you. *I was made for more than this. I've gained all the benefit I can from alcohol. Now I need to look beyond alcohol for something that will satisfy a deeper hunger and quench a deeper thirst.* You're ready for living water.

Chapter 14 — Stage 3: Crisis Focused

When you're in pain, will you reach for a spiritual answer, or will you return to the physical? Can you embrace a spiritual worldview and move toward God? Do you consider Him friend or foe?

The crisis mode is a time of internal exploration brought about by positive or negative crises in your life. You must overcome challenges and reconcile with the three attitudes toward God defined in Chapter 4 (Allied, Against, Avoiding). Do you accept or reject the reality presented to you? Do you reject or accept who you are? Your experiences will hopefully lead you toward God instead of away from God. You can look for a solution to suffering and learn how to use crises for growth.

Recognize an Unhealthy Focus

Everyone has a worldview whether they're aware of it or not. When a person can't resolve her crisis, she will create a worldview that goes against a biblical worldview (see Chapter 3 to review worldviews). An unhealthy belief system ultimately replaces God with self-effort. An independent adult will attempt to make life work on her own.

An unhealthy independent person controls with a tight fist and seizes what she wants. This forcing approach uses creation the wrong way. Confidence comes not from things, but from the Maker of things.

The following two examples have in common a fierce independence. The independence goes too far, though, leaving God out of the equation of life. The radical is against God, while the hard-worker avoids God.

The Blinded Radical

Anger drives the radical to pursue autonomy. He'll adopt any worldview that provides an alternative to Christianity. The radical's primary worth is based upon recreating himself in his own image. He rejects God's absolute design but is mature in the sense that he has built a self-image around who he wants to be. He rejects an ongoing relationship with his Creator. Of all the caricatures, he has the most antagonistic relationship with God and His followers.

The Isolated Hard-Worker

The hard-worker's primary worth is based upon self-sufficiency. Her worldview leans toward humanism. She has learned to expect disappointment from relationships. She's all about responsibility with minimal relationship. She's a responsible drifter in need of social interaction—but she strives to avoid any reliance on other people. While she's not against God, she has a weak connection to God. Because she distrusts God so much, her intimacy with God is almost non-existent. Samantha is an example of this kind of person who grows up yet remains distant from God (see Chapter 9).

Correct an Unhealthy Focus

To resolve the crisis and become Christ focused, you must work through your doubt. You'll need to do these three things:
1. **Detox from idolizing creation.** Shift your focus from making life better outside of yourself to making life better inside of yourself.
2. **Believe God is good.** Clarify your God-image by putting your faith in what the Bible says is true, and cultivating more positive experiences with God.
3. **Pursue your identity.** Understand your identity as separate from creation and God. You have your own separate identity apart from your friends, your addictions, and even from God. You're free to decide how you want to live—subject to the reality God provides, of course.

Detox from Idolizing Creation

To search for meaning and purpose, you must temporarily give up external productivity. Instead of focusing on what you can do, you need to learn how to be. Allow God to be your caregiver.

As you detox from using creation the wrong way, you become newly aware of your legitimate desires. You feel your desire for God to meet your core longings. Your basic emotional needs for approval and acceptance allow you to make the decision to move toward God.

A firm knowledge of your identity allows you to enjoy creation without worshiping creation. You can have your cake and eat it too when you prove you don't need it in the first place. This is a paradox of maturity. When you prove you don't need something, you prove you can use it the right way: responsibly, with appropriate restraint. You prove that when you have it, you won't let it destroy you. This is like driving a car with a powerful engine. If you don't know how to use it, you could crash and burn. But when you do know how to use it, you can enjoy it for all it's worth. All our drives work this way. We must tame our impulses regarding food, for example, or sex, or the desire to be significant.

Believe God is Good

In your heart, do you consider God to be your friend or your enemy? When you consider that God is a real person, you must grapple with who He is. Can you develop a cohesive worldview that includes a loving God? Or is the world too full of evil for a loving God to be real? Do you accept or reject God's reality? If you want to continue to grow, you'll need to come to terms with what you'll do with God.

If you choose a positive view, this means you trust God's goodness and seek alignment with God. If you choose a negative view, this means you doubt God's goodness and move away from or against God.

To overcome your crisis, you must stop thinking that your experiences define who God is. Instead, you must ask, *How do my experiences falsely define who I am and who God is?*

Job remained faithful to God even when he suffered. He lost everything but his life and his wife. He was able to endure suffering because he trusted God was in control of the situation. Although he was in great pain, he never stopped trusting God.[19] His perseverance paid off.

> *"God may kill me,*
> *but still I will trust him and offer my defense."*
> —Job 13:15 (CEV)

How can you reach contentment? By using creation according to its God-given capacity—your capacity included. And by expecting life to include suffering. To lose weight, you have to tolerate feeling hungry. To maintain proper boundaries with people, you might have to tolerate feeling lonely on occasion.

Suffering can feel intolerable, but it isn't avoidable, or at least it shouldn't be. You suffer because feeling permanently content is impossible. If God chooses for you to suffer for Him greatly in this life, God will honor you in the next life (Romans 8:17).

Knowing the truth helps you endure, staying available to bring about positive change, thereby helping others to endure. By placing hope in God and the life to come, you'll find it easier to accept pain and shortfall in this life.

Carl Jung said, "Neurosis is always a substitute for legitimate suffering."[20] You may not know why you're suffering, but you suffer either way. You're better off, then, to embrace suffering with your eyes wide open. If you refuse to make the necessary and difficult life changes to eliminate the problem at the root, you're choosing to continue to suffer anxiety or other types of emotional distress. You can have a healthy root by aligning yourself to God's design and developing the character needed to endures life's challenges.

God and His truth are a constant when all else fails. When you're mistreated, God is aware of your suffering. Egypt enslaved the Israelites for 400 years. People died in the desert, but God didn't love them less despite their difficult circumstances. This truth should challenge your worldview and image of God. The big picture doesn't change even when your circumstances change. Suffering is meaningful, but fulfilling God's purposes is more meaningful.

Disappointments are inevitable, but you can develop resilience. Find a truth that you're willing to uphold and defend passionately. Don't try to shelter yourself from disappointments. Step through your disappointments; move forward in spite of them so you can fulfill your life purpose.

Pursue Your Identity

Experience the joy of aligning your self-image with your identity. As you mature into who God made you to be, you become more resilient. You can be full of joy as you rely on God instead of on circumstances. You're able to persevere through a season of suffering.

To experience your identity, you'll need to understand two psychological terms: *integration* and *differentiation*. They're big words, but they're important and simple enough to understand.

Integration

Integration is the process of restoring order to chaos and bringing harmony where there is conflict. You need to be integrated because an unresolved crisis is messy and harmful. A crisis can be as caustic to self-image as acid is to metal. Integration brings the various parts of your life into harmony, restoring their strength and vitality.

The physical becomes integrated with the spiritual, for example, when you use your body as an instrument of righteousness instead of wickedness (Romans 6:13). And your emotional reality becomes integrated with your cognitive reality when you can feel and express your pain while also continuing to act like a responsible adult.

Differentiation

Differentiation is the process of clarifying how you're unique. When you differentiate, you become more aware of who you are and how you're separate from others. For example, you realize your feelings are your own, no one else can feel them, and no one else is responsible for them. When a mom is cold, she might tell her child to dress warmer. Or you've probably heard the saying, *If momma isn't happy, no one is happy.* Of course, moms understand differentiation, so I'm having some fun with this, but children don't. When a young child is cold, he believes everyone else is too.

You're part of a community, but you are your own person completely. You're born dependent on your mom, but a separate person. What you want, others might not want. But you can appeal to God and others, seeking to influence them in a healthy negotiation of meeting needs. You'll want to be separated from and connected to a community at the same time.

TO IDENTITY AND BEYOND

Plan to Be Christ Focused

You'll end up in crisis mode when your worldview breaks. Your understanding of reality can become obselete when negative life experiences dominate your positive life experiences. In these moments of crisis, can you trust God? You might no longer be dependent on your caregiver but continue to choose stubborn independence from God. Resolving the crisis favorably involves reconciling your external experiences with your internal reality, and your internal reality with God's reality.

God's Reality

God	Creation
	(Your Identity)

In Chapter 3 you learned that God's reality consists of God and creation, which includes your identity. Your reality is a shadow of God's reality. You can't see God's reality as clearly as you'd like.

Your Reality, Perceptions, Worldview

God-View	Interpretation of Experiences
	(Self-Image)

Build trust with God by allowing positive experiences with God to override the effects of negative experiences. Try a simple prayer. *God, I'm struggling to believe You're good. If I'm honest, I feel like You failed to keep me safe when I got into that car accident. Please help me see Your goodness despite the pain I'm in.* Pay attention afterward to what God does in your life in the coming days and weeks. If you continue to struggle, you might need to expand on this prayer by writing a lament.[21] You'll know you're successful when your new worldview is sophisticated enough to explain your life experiences and hold true to a biblical worldview.

This process will prove that you have an identity and prompt you to go on discovering, defining, and understanding it.

Check If You're Stuck in Crisis Mode

If you're stuck in crisis, you've chosen a path of isolation from God. You exclude God from your life because you're unable to trust Him. You've separated from God and others to form your identity, but you've failed to develop the part of your identity that allows you to join together with God. In crisis mode, you fail to resolve your crisis in a positive way, so any of the following might be true:

- You idolize creation and return to it for comfort.
- You continue to reinvent yourself in radical (non-biblical) ways.
- You fail to internalize a sense of contentment with who you are and your place in life.
- You lose interest in creating a more sophisticated worldview.
- You reject God because you reject yourself.
- You settle on a self-image that doesn't reflect your true God-given identity.
- You refuse to accept God and join together with Him.

Implement Solutions for Becoming Unstuck

Your emotionally wounded, needy, and sometimes sinful self needs God's love as much as your healthy self does. The best way to experience joy is to explore your identity and purpose—to begin to know yourself the way God knows you. This is a difficult journey. You need internal motivation to get moving. Sometimes you need to seed your life with small successes to build motivation.

- Embrace your crisis; don't run from it.
- Seek healing from emotional wounds.

- Experience the joy of developing your identity.
- Increase your faith in God so you can see Him as good.
- Resolve that God is the only way forward.
- Consume again. Allow God to be your caregiver. Pursue self-care. Breathe. Take in what you need to thrive.

Check If You're Ready to Be Christ Focused

As a healthy person, you'll have resolved your crisis, gaining new insight into your meaning, purpose, and definition. You have a clear answer to the three main questions:
1. Who is God?
2. Who am I?
3. What is the nature of creation?

You're ready to be Christ focused because you embrace a Christian worldview:
1. God's identity: *I worship God as holy and believe he's the exclusive source of anything good.*
2. Your identity: *God loves me as He made me to be and I have a distinct purpose.*
3. Creation's identity: *I enjoy creation only for what God meant it to be.*

And you declare that the following points are true:
- *I look to God for meaning.*
- *I desire to commit to allying with God.*
- *I will believe and follow God even when life doesn't turn out well.*

If you're not ready to ally with God yet, you won't be able to grasp how your identity works with God. You may want independence and internal satisfaction, but this won't do you much good if you won't join with God. You can seek to develop an identity, but your attempts in isolation from God will only cause you to drift away from Him.

If you desire to ally with God, you'll move on to become Christ focused. You'll seek understanding of God and His creation, and

Chapter 14 — Stage 3: Crisis Focused

you'll begin to live according to the truth. Any crisis of faith in creation will lead you to strengthen your faith in God.

Study Questions

1. Close your eyes; picture God. Now write down all the words that honestly describe who you know God to be. Don't just write down Bible verses; choose words based on your life experience of God. Notice the tension between your experiences and the truth in the Bible.
2. How much do you trust or distrust God?
3. How has your perspective amid crisis and suffering changed?
4. Describe your current worldview, God-view, and self-image. Write a paragraph (3 to 5 sentences) for each.

---

19 Consider https://www.gotquestions.org/though-slay-trust-Him.html for more details.

20 Carl Jung, Psychology and Religion (New York: Yale University Press, 1938). Also see https://counsellingresource.com/features/2010/08/03/jung-words-of-wisdom.

21 See my book *Confident Identity* for detailed exercises for working through negative feelings toward God, including how to write your own Psalm of lament.

Chapter 15

Stage 4: Christ Focused

If you're in Stage 4, you've moved past needing a caregiver, and you're able to enjoy creation and be productive. You've confronted your identity crisis, and you've emerged with faith in God and a Christian worldview. A healthy Christian isn't stuck avoiding or moving against God. Instead, she honestly seeks Jesus. She reconciles her experiences by correcting any negative views of God so she can move forward in good faith.

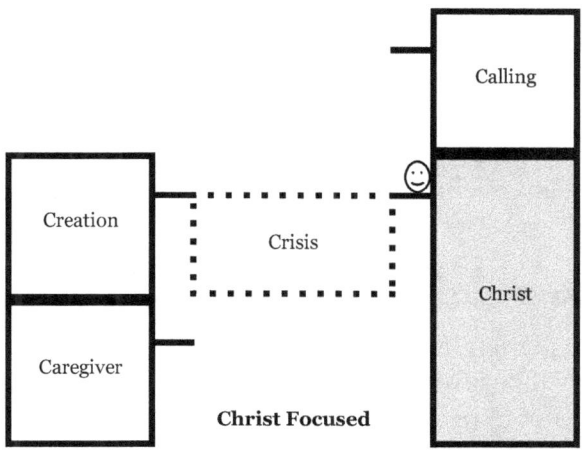

Christ Focused

After the decision to ally with God, you need to continue to explore the depths of who you are. If during your crisis you were "dating God," now you're "engaged to God."[22] Christians and non-Christians alike must spend time in the first three stages—but to be Christ focused, you must be a Christian.

A Christ-focused believer will pass through the three steps of the gentle climb to loving God (see Chapter 7). A Christian worships God and enjoys His goodness. As a Christian, you can be content even when life disappoints. Your contentment becomes a permanent part of who you are. God fills you up. Therefore, you aren't always trying to get more from life.

This doesn't mean you'll be perfect, nor that you'll experience life as heaven on earth. As a Christian, you'll still have to be intentional about living a Christ-focused, authentic life.

Authentic living means discovering and pursuing all God made you to be, steadily increasing in integrity. How you appear to others is in alignment with both your self-image (who you think you are) and your identity (who God knows you are). This alignment ensures that you won't compromise who you are in order to please others.

You realize that the spirit is willing, but the flesh is weak (Matthew 26:41). However, you're fully invested in this new life of cooperation with God.

As a healthy person, you commit to authentic living for God:
- You desire to find the real you and eliminate all that is the fake you.
- Joining with God is truly your heart's desire.
- You align yourself to God's reality and act upon His truth.
- You worship your Creator, not His creation.
- You sense being passionate ("on fire") for God.

Recognize an Unhealthy Focus

Christians struggle with two problems with respect to identity. They dismiss their own sin and stop growing, or they use humility as an excuse not to reach their full potential in Christ.

Don't Stop Growing

As a Christian, your identity is fully established as a saint, but you're still stuck with your flesh. You're still capable of sin even though you can consider yourself dead to sin and alive in Christ.

We know that Christ, being raised from the dead, will never die again; death no longer has dominion over him. For the death he died he died to sin, once for all, but the life he lives he lives to God. So you also must consider

Chapter 15 — Stage 4: Christ Focused

> *yourselves dead to sin and*
> *alive to God in Christ Jesus.*
> —Romans 6:9–11

You'll never want to stop being Christ-focused. Yet, since faith without works is dead, a healthy Christian will also be calling-focused (James 2:17). You'll look to Christ, receive His love and care, and then do what the Father is doing (John 5:19).

An unhealthy Christian will stop growing in truth and grace. She'll use her freedom in Christ and return to a previous stage of being creation or caregiver focused.

All Christians will sin. At times, we may doubt God during the trials God brings our way. We can become temporarily lost in sin. But a true-believer won't remain hopelessly stuck in doubt or sin—not because she suddenly finds the missing resolve, but because God is working in her to make her Christlike.

Don't Lose Your Identity

You can give up your sin, and you can give up your life in sacrificial service, but don't give up your identity.

A Christian is a dwelling place for God and is complete as an individual man or woman. However, together with God, you can accomplish more—just like a man and a woman can accomplish more together. To fully experience your union with God, you must first experience yourself as a separate, well-defined individual—just as God separated woman from man before He joined them back together in marriage.

When you become a Christian and are passionate for God, you want to spend all your time with Him—in the Word, in prayer, and worshiping Him. You may even think that you have the same mission as Jesus—to save the lost.

Jesus talks about believers being as branches that are grafted into a Vine—which is Himself. As a new Christian, you might feel as though you have the same purpose as the Vine. But for you to join God in a healthy way, you must first understand your identity in God as a separate person with a separate calling. Sure, you're still called to be in the world and influencing the world for good. But your calling is separate from God's and different from everyone else's.

Correct an Unhealthy Focus

Beyond Identity in Christ

Everyone has an identity. Only Christians can base their identity in Christ, which means to define one's self-image based on God's reality. But this doesn't mean you lose your distinctiveness when you become a Christian. Only you have your unique identity.

God wants us to imitate Christ and other healthy Christ followers, but we can't replicate Christ's identity or obliterate our own. We clothe ourselves with Christ, but we don't disguise ourselves. We gain Christ's holiness and retain our personality. Being a part of a body means we're not all ears or eyes or feet and definitely not all heads. There is only one head, which is Christ.

You don't glorify God by acting identically to Christ; you glorify God by fulfilling God's unique purpose and calling for your life. Christ can't fulfill your purpose for you; it's a partnership. Christ's death and resurrection allow you to fulfill your destiny. Christ is both a perfect model and also a prototype as the first perfected human, one of many more to come.

In C.S. Lewis's book *The Screwtape Letters*, the demon Wormwood's uncle says, "Our war aim is a world in which Our Father Below has drawn all other beings into himself: the Enemy wants a world full of beings united to Him but still distinct."[23] Even demons know that people have their own distinct identity. The Christian band MercyMe wrote a song in 2014 called "More of You and Less of Me." This doesn't mean we are to have less of an identity, but we should desire to sin less and be more holy.

Jesus is both human and God. You're Jesus's brother or sister. Siblings are similar, but not identical. You're made in God's image, but you're also totally one of a kind. Your identity is on par with Jesus's identity in that you're made in God's image. You have the Holy Spirit like Jesus does, but you're also a new creation having a purpose different from Jesus.

As a new creation, you've gained access to your identity in Christ. Your identity hasn't changed, but you now have the ability to align your self-image with your true identity—the one God predestined and keeps safely stored in His creative mind.

Your identity in Christ includes the standard features. For example, every Christian has a relationship with God and has eternal life. These are amazing gifts! They make you distinct from non-Christians, but they don't in themselves define you. There are many Christians with the gift of teaching, but each one teaches a different way. There are many Christians with the ability to sing, but each one inspires worship differently. There are many pastors, but each one communicates the Gospel in his own way. God inspired the Bible, but each biblical author put his own style into the writing. God special-orders every one of His children. It's to your advantage to know what makes you unique among all people, including other Christians.

Be Powerful

After you've clarified who you are, you're ready to explore your potential as God's ally. How have you been uniquely crafted to accomplish God's plans? This is where the fun and excitement in life begins. You start learning who you are the day you're born (physically), and you start a new type of learning the day you're born again (spiritually). This is a never-ending journey—certainly in this life and probably into eternity—because God is both knowable and infinite.

You can't define yourself without referring to God. You're not just a nurse, you're a Christian nurse. You're not just a business owner, you're a Christian business owner. Your identity is fundamentally tied to being a Christian first, then whatever makes you unique. So you should pursue a joyful union with God. By teaming with God, you live in the sweet spot of fulling your purpose. You become *you* raised exponentially to the power of God, able to do greater works beyond what Jesus accomplished (John 14:12).

When God dwells with you, He doesn't overshadow you. He doesn't take over your brain like a parasitic alien. He provides spiritual power that brings life to your unique identity.

To live authentically means to live according to God's original intentions for creating you, not others' opinions or desires. Your identity includes a close partnership with God through the Holy Spirit living in you. Your identity joined with God's identity allows you to interact with reality a whole new way.

With God's presence, the ordinary can become extraordinary. A fiddle sounds better in God's hands than in anyone else's hands. Who you are in God's hands defines the real you. Be encouraged by the value He places on you. Place yourself into God's hands.

Walking in partnership with God maximizes your potential in every way. You can't stay addicted to something and become close to God. The more you favor your drug of choice, the less you can see God. However, you can make God your drug of choice and be powered by God.

Rebel Against Who You Aren't

When you become a Christian and you put yourself in God's hands, He may want to play you like a fiddle, but you're used to being treated like a jackhammer. Maybe you have always been rough around the edges, but it turns out you're not who you think you are. Everyone has an identity. Some are undiscovered, underdeveloped, or mislabeled.

To be genuinely you in Christ without shame, you need to be able to unmask yourself in authentic living. Jesus says you're salt and light, and as such you shouldn't remain hidden (Matthew 5:13–16).

A Christ-focused identity lives in the light. A false identity hides in the darkness. Some people don't know who God made them to be; they would prefer to assume the identity of who they want to be. Unfortunately, the two aren't the same, which creates a lot of confusion. Pretending to be someone you're not only makes life more difficult.

Why do you wear false coverings? Is it because nobody seems to appreciate who you really are? Are you pretending to be someone you're not, like an introvert meeting the demands of an extroverted world?

You wear a mask to cover your wounds—the parts you're ashamed of. You might not realize how much of you really isn't you. You can be deceived into being comfortable in the wrong skin! Can you rescue and resuscitate the true you buried beneath the false you?

The more you retain your false identity, the more you'll divide yourself into a public and a private self. The public self hides the dysfunctional parts and therefore appears better than average. Only the individual owner knows his private self is worse than average. To be whole again, you must bring who you think and feel you are into contact with the truth. The goal is to accept how you really are—how God made you.

There is an inward force, the truth, that drives you to accept reality. And there is a corresponding force, evil, that attempts to hide the truth. Hiding the truth involves stating untruths such as "You won't die if you eat, but you'll be like God" (Genesis 3:1–5). It also includes negative experiences that teach you false ideas that seem true at the time, such as "I'm worthless because my father yells at me."

When you're joined to God, you're free to be exactly who God made you to be, without the masks. Living authentically means to live without masks and shame. To find the real you, stop believing the lies you tell yourself about who you are. Then include in your self-image all that God says you are.

To find your true identity and embrace who God says you are, you must also rebel against who you aren't. You've tried things and concluded, *That's not for me*. For example, *I tried singing in the choir, and now I know that's not how God has gifted me*. Healthy rebellion harms no one and moves your self-image closer to your true identity. Rebel against others who want you to be someone other than who God made you to be. Put off your old self so there is room for your new self to shine (Ephesians 4:22–24).

Put off being pushy, rude, and devious. Put off trying to function as a hand if God made you an eye. Put off pretending to be a foot if God made you an ear. You should find it apparent what God doesn't want you to be. So rebel against these things. God is the only one who can fully show you who you really are. Trust Him always and follow His lead.

Everybody wears something; you can't be naked. But you can remove the layers of fake until you get to the real you. If you find it hard to tell what is truly you, align your thinking with God's design. Adam and Eve were originally naked and unashamed (Genesis 2:25). Confront your shame. Enter the fight to reclaim your right to be exactly who God made you to be.

While rebelling, you have two guardrails to keep your expectations realistic. One is your current understanding of who you are (don't regress and become less mature). The other is the limitations of who God designed you to be (don't go beyond His intentional design). To fully rebel, you must also change your worldview when it's wrong. Always be ready to adjust your worldview to be closer to God's reality.

Be Comfortable in Your Own Skin

After you come to know what you aren't made for and rebel against those things, it's time to discover what you are made for. What comes naturally to you, without forced effort? Are you comfortable with Plain You, without the bells and whistles?

You must accept yourself exactly as you are. Stop performing. Stop pretending. Stop trying to be more than. Stop feeling less than. Stop looking for your worth in what you do. God accepts you completely and exactly as you are. Stop right now. Do you feel God's total acceptance? Can you feel your longing for His acceptance?

Who is Plain You? Is Plain You good enough? You have a unique design, full of value God wants you to explore. What will happen if you start doing what comes naturally and instinctively to you instead of what others have programmed you to do? What would your life be like if you still believed everything you were told as a child? You don't still believe in Santa Claus, do you?

Being who others want you to be instead of who God made you to be is called people-pleasing. Every interaction you have with the pit of pleasing others will fall into one of these categories:

Chapter 15 — Stage 4: Christ Focused

1. You fall into the pit. You didn't see it coming. You're confused. You have no idea who you are.
2. You fall into the pit. You saw it coming but couldn't avoid it. You're ashamed. You don't like who you are.
3. You fall into the pit. You saw it coming and walked in anyway. You're frustrated. You wonder who you are.
4. You see the pit. You avoid the pit. You're healthy. You're learning to like who you are.
5. You no longer go near the pit. You're healed. You love who you are.[24]

You need constant vigilance to escape and stay out of the pit of pleasing the world. You need to become aware of the truth of who you are and who God is. The pit becomes easier to avoid as you mature. Just like David, you can't wear Saul's armor. You have to fulfill your purpose within the bounds of how God designed you (1 Samuel 17:38–40).

Seek to Please God

The best way to live authentically is to please God. What will happen if you stop trying to be who others need or want you to be? You might feel out of place or useless for a while.

Some people might get angry with you when you decide to please God instead of them. You might need to stop giving in one way to start giving elsewhere in order to align yourself with God's purposes. Maybe you'll stop volunteering at a homeless shelter so you can have more time with your kids. Or maybe you'll leave work on time so you can attend a Bible study. Or maybe you'll stop watching your sister's kids so you can volunteer at a homeless shelter.

You can either please God or please man (Galatians 1:10). You must face this ultimatum at some point in your life to continue growing. Other people may not approve of your choice, but Jesus is your boss, not your co-workers or your friends or your neighbors. Don't adjust yourself to what others want. Measure who you think or feel you are against who God made you to be.

If you're pleasing God, you won't worry about what others think, and you won't compare yourself to others. Some comparison is good, and some is bad. Healthy comparison is seeing how you're different without concluding you're more or less valuable. This allows you to focus on *your* potential without bragging, boasting, or putting anybody down. You can celebrate others' positive differences as much as or more than your own.

When you compare yourself to others in an unhealthy way, you do so because you don't feel valued. Don't measure yourself against another person as Peter did with John.

> *Peter turned and saw the disciple whom Jesus loved following them, ... When Peter saw him, he said to Jesus, "Lord, what about this man?" Jesus said to him, "If it is my will that he remain until I come, what is that to you? You follow me!"*
> —John 21:20–22

Harmful attitudes that arise in the midst of comparison include jealousy, envy, competitiveness, compensation (overplaying strengths), and rejection. All of these allow external reality to define internal worth.

This explains sibling rivalry, or the need to be special. If you allow yourself to feel redundant or commonplace, you won't be able to acknowledge the value God has put within you. Instead of feeling like Plain You isn't good enough, you need to see your unique contribution—the destiny God has planned for you. Don't define yourself based on what you see others doing. Do your own thing based on God's instructions to you.

There is good rejection (God accepts you, man rejects you, but you accept you) and bad rejection (God accepts you, man rejects you, and you reject you because you don't believe that God feels differently). Being rejected from the company of certain people might be a positive development. But you won't be able to see the situation in a positive light if you base your value on the recognition you receive from others.

Have courage to travel the road God has for you—the journey no one else can take. God has that road reserved exclusively for you. You can travel it and produce works that no one else can.

Plan to Be Calling Focused

Check If You're Stuck Focusing on Christ

You're stuck focusing on Christ when you struggle with the climb to loving God. You need more practice receiving and needing God.

- You trust God to save you, but you're afraid of losing your salvation.
- You can't feel God's unconditional acceptance.
- You don't want to risk exercising your faith by using your spiritual gifts.
- You compare yourself to others because you don't know your value.

Implement Solutions for Becoming Unstuck

Try any of the following:
- Spend time alone with God to feel God's acceptance and develop self-acceptance.
- Ask your pastor for opportunities to serve in a variety of situations. Then determine which ones fit better with your identity.
- Take some spiritual gift tests.
- Review the description of the people-pleasing pit to make sure you're not trapped in it.
- Pray, asking God to help you see your specific calling.

Check If You're Ready to Be Calling Focused

As a healthy Christian, you should not only have experienced God's love for you, but also God walking alongside you during difficult trials.

You're ready to be calling focused when
- you have a real relationship with God: *I know the truth in my head and I know God in my heart;* and

- you trust God: *God has been faithful to me. I trust Him even when I suffer.*

And these characteristics should also be true:
- You feel a growing sense of who you are and can give to others from the overflow you're receiving.
- You desire to join with others to accomplish more than you can by yourself.
- You sense the fullness of God's way, and you want to contribute to His cause.
- You're willing to give up earthly success for eternal treasure.
- You want to live out your days with purpose.
- You have a preliminary sense of your purpose and calling.

Consider how much of your life is centered on making life convenient for others at your expense. This can be healthy behavior, provided you already know who you are. A mom getting up multiple times a night to care for a child bends herself to the child's schedule. A man doing exactly what his company needs provides for the company and his family.

But these acts, though necessary and noble, don't comprise a person's identity. At some point, you must reach a deeper awareness of God's ideal design and purpose for your life. If you're living out that purpose by being a mom, keep at it. If you're fulfilling your purpose by working for your company, keep at it.

Being responsible is part of a Christian identity, so don't quit your day job unless God urges you to, and you have enough faith. God may want you to keep working even in a place where you're uncomfortable. If so, that is your calling; keep at it.

But don't ignore a greater calling to your true purpose even if it threatens to disrupt your life, or if other people would disapprove. Others don't own you. Only God owns you. Is your calling coming from the mouths of men or from the mouth of God?

Are you living the authentic life God wants you to live, or are you living a life that He doesn't support, a life that only meets others' needs and wants? Perhaps you're already serving God by supporting another's calling. But this may be insufficient. You can't fulfill God's purpose for your life by ignoring any of your God-given potential.

Your destiny awaits—your adventure begins. Throw off what is holding you back from reaching your potential and your purpose. In this life, even with God's blessing, you won't reach a permanent place of bliss. That's called heaven. But you can find contentment when you accept your God-given identity, your life circumstances, and God's responsibility for the outcomes.

Study Questions

1. Define who you are as Plain You. How much do you like Plain You?
2. Have you ever felt like an imposter? Imposter syndrome is the condition of believing you don't live up to your own good reputation.
3. What parts of your authentic self are you suppressing or ignoring? In what way can you grow toward your authentic self today?
4. In what ways do you act to please people, and in what ways do you act to please God? How often are these at odds with each other?
5. What is God's role (responsibility) and what is your role (responsibility) in your Christian walk?
6. Enter into a time of contemplative prayer. Ask yourself, "Who am I?" and as you consider the answer, don't include the problems you're currently struggling with.
7. Make two lists: "Who I am" and "Who I'm not."
8. Read the poem *The Touch of the Master's Hand* by Myra Brooks Welch.

---

[22] Only when we're all heaven will we, as the bride of Christ, be "married to God."

[23] C. S. Lewis, *The Screwtape Letters* (London: Geoffrey Bles, 1942), Chapter VIII.

[24] The idea for the five categories of the people-pleasing pit are a result of my familiarity with Autobiography in Five Short Chapters by Portia Nelson.

Chapter 16

Stage 5: Calling Focused

When you learn to live authentically in your Christ-focused identity, you'll be ready to move onward and upward toward your destiny. But keep in mind, being allied with God doesn't mean life will be easy all the time.

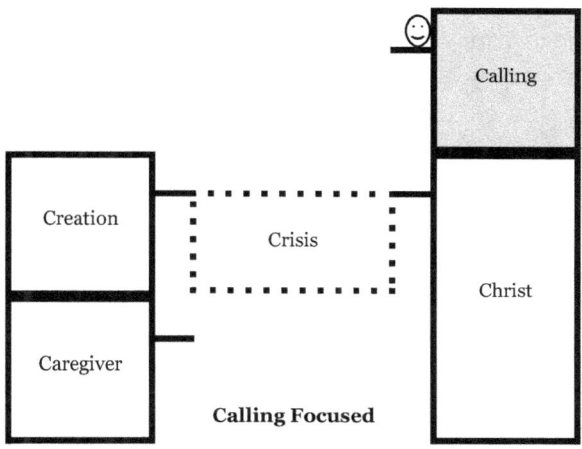

Pursuing your destiny is a journey, and one God has for all of us. We must determine to know with more certainty what God has to say about our lives. In a sense, we're all doubting Thomases, and we need to continually preach to ourselves the truth deep within. Peter denied he knew God at first, but eventually he chose death over denial. That's a profound transformation from doubt to confident conviction. Peter knew Jesus as a real person both before and after the resurrection. He moved on to write the books of First and Second Peter, refused to deny the truth, and died a martyr.

When you seek God, rebel against your false identity, embrace your true identity, and pursue your destiny, others won't recognize who you are for a while. They often won't understand why you need to change. They won't be able to accept your new priorities and purpose. They'll still want to be consumers of the old you. But keep living out your destiny, and they will either fall out of your life or come to terms with the new you.

When going through the emotional pain of being resented and rejected for shifting your priorities, redouble your efforts to learn your true identity. Learning your identity will

- maximize your life satisfaction—you'll enjoy life more;
- help you see God's will—you'll have a definite direction to pursue;
- encourage you to give up worldly fulfillment to accomplish God's purposes;
- increase your peace and reduce your stress—you'll have less to worry about; and
- bring you closer to God—knowing yourself helps you know God.

As an addict recovers and becomes sober, he can take a defensive, preventative stance. He could forever invest all his energy into avoiding addiction. However, his recovery is only half complete if he only prevents bad things from happening. What good things is he going to accomplish? He needs to venture into the positive area of identity growth. He'll then be able to help others through the gifts God gave him.

An inescapable reality and an intentional identity lead to an inevitable destiny.

Much of life is already determined by God. This fact should make it easier for you to conclude that God also had a specific purpose in mind when He created you. You have a destiny—even though you might not be able to see all its implications.

Faith fuels destiny. When you have faith, you can live out your destiny without worrying about the momentary outcomes. Abraham persevered in faith to the end of his life, but he never saw the complete impact of God's promise to him (Hebrews 11:13–16). Keep in the back of your mind that the same might be true for you.

While you're here on earth, you have a clear purpose and destiny to fulfill. Intentionally seeking to discover your part is the fastest way for God's plan to come to fruition. Act on God's side. Carry out

His orders. Instead of just trying to endure your trials, go on the offensive.

Are You a Drifter or a Pursuer?

A sailor woke up on his ship adrift in the ocean. He didn't know where he was. He didn't remember how he got there. He couldn't recall where he came from. He had no idea where he was going.

He did have a knowledge of sailing. All directions looked the same to him, so he continued to sail in the direction he was already going. He eventually found land and settled there, adopting the customs of the native culture. But the feeling that he didn't belong never left him for the rest of his life.

Does this sound like your life's journey so far?

Experienced sailors use the sun and other stars—fixed objects in the sky—to navigate the ocean. They position their ships so the wind can push them. Without a relationship with God, you're like a sailor without the sun and wind. Without an identity, you're like a sailor without a ship.

You need to stop and examine the course you're setting with your life. Are you moving in a particular direction on purpose? Or do you passively let the ocean currents take you further out to sea?

---

*If you don't know where you're going,
any road will get you there.*
—Lewis Carroll

If your only goal is not to be where you are, then why should you waste time trying to pick the best direction? If you want to get away fast, why should you bother analyzing your options? You can just pick any direction and go.

Drifting along in life is the only option when you have no clue who you are. Trial and error are acceptable. But drifting without a systematic mapping of your journey is foolish. If you don't learn from your mistakes, you're doomed to repeat them.

> *If one does not know to which port one is sailing,*
> *no wind is favorable.*
> —Seneca

If you don't care where you're going, why would you care which way the wind is blowing? If you don't have a goal or destination in mind, no help exists for you. Nothing will improve your situation until you determine to set a clear course.

Immaturity is drifting along without paying attention to where you've been. Do you want to be a drifter, or do you want to live with purpose and meaning? Maturity is growing in the knowledge and experience of who God is and who you are.

The Good News

We have covered a lot and come a long way. We have seen how many people haven't made the effort to discover their true identity. Their self-image remains far from who they truly are. But they long to be loved, significant, and tied to something greater than themselves. Depression, anxiety, and loneliness dominate the headlines. People seek to fill the hole inside with work or drugs or sex or relationships. People pursue just about anything in creation to experience spiritual satisfaction. The enemy—the devil—is all too happy to encourage the lie that you can be fulfilled through these things. But you have learned the truth: the emptiness inside comes from not knowing why you exist, and perhaps more importantly who created you. Now you're on the path to fulfillment. Now that you have a relationship with the Creator God, you can pursue your destiny.

Your Identity is Your Compass

As you journey through life, God is your true north. If you want to be intentional about your journey, you must set your compass to point to true north—to the God who will lead your path. The more your self-image aligns with your identity, the more your identity points to God.

God wants you to map your experiences and make increasingly educated decisions about your life direction and goals. Your identity allows you to find your way. In knowing your identity, you can define the meaning of your life. As you understand who you are, you're able to move with confidence and purpose.

How can you make this journey? Let's remember what we've learned:

All Christians Should Learn Their Identity

You'll never completely know every aspect of who God made you to be in this life, so there's always room to grow. Be persistent in pursuing your identity.

Identity is what something is, as distinguishable from everything else. Confidence is the assurance of something. To have a confident identity means to live with the assurance of knowing who you are. You come to know yourself, and you're not ashamed anymore. Your identity does you no good when it is hidden, nor when it's discovered but not appreciated, embraced, and put into play. To function with your confident identity, you must continuously improve your awareness and acceptance of your identity, revealing a unique set of actions that will ultimately further God's kingdom.

You're a One-of-a-Kind Unique Creation

God doesn't make duplicates. Instead, He crafts each individual for a specific purpose.

Identity has many different facets:
- Who you are according to God. God created you with intention, and His definition is your true identity.
- The set of characteristics by which you're definitively recognizable. You're easily distinguished from others.
- Your unique characteristics held by no other person. You have something that no one else will ever have.
- What remains the same, constant, persisting over time, under varying circumstances. Whatever is part of you is permanently yours, or else it really isn't part of you.

You're Distinct Even Among All Other Christians

When you became a Christian, you identified with Christ, but you didn't become Christ. Jesus has His identity as God and human. You can't have His identity. You can't be God. You aren't an anonymous, indistinct follower of Christ.

Your goal in life isn't to become a Jesus clone. Instead of trying to mimic Jesus's personality, God wants you to be a distinct personality that demonstrates the same character as Jesus.

You Experience and Exhibit God Like No One Else Can

You're irreplaceable. Others will appreciate Jesus more when they see a distinct person exhibiting His character than if they see a generic person trying to show love. God wants cooperation, diversity, and unity. God delights in seeing Himself reflected in the many different identities of His people. God is glorified when we reflect His character.

You Relate to God and Use Creation the Right Way

The surest path to closeness with God is to allow God to restore you to His intentions. You can be authentic to God's original design. When you align yourself with your Creator's intent, you maximize your potential and your life satisfaction.

You See Your Eternal Identity by Faith

As you see reality from God's perspective and taste His goodness, you're on the path to your true identity. God allows you to look not only with your physical eyes but with His spiritual eyes. Once you're born again, you'll live out your true identity with God forever.

You Build Your Self-Image on Who God Says You Are

You can't lose your identity. Anything you can lose isn't part of your identity. Your identity doesn't consist of your job, possessions, or relationships. So don't build your self-image on anything you can lose.

You Accept Jesus's Sacrifice

You can't become Christ, but you can accept His sacrificial death to enable you to become all God made you to be. You can base your value on Jesus's sacrifice.

You Accept the Holy Spirit's Presence and Help

You have a God-shaped hole in your heart. As a Christian, you have God's Holy Spirit living within you. The Spirit enables you to grow spiritually and exhibit Christlike behavior.

You Enjoy Abundant Life

God created and called His work good. He wants you to enjoy what He has provided. You can freely pursue pleasure as long as it doesn't interfere with building God's kingdom. Love God and do what you want.

You Play the Long Game

God calls you to serve others as you mature. However, you can't accomplish this until you first receive from others. You can't sustain giving from a place of emptiness. You must constantly invest time and energy into the pursuit of healing as you seek to forgive yourself and others.

You Advance God's Kingdom

If you want to be effective for the kingdom of God and maximize your life satisfaction, the only option you have is to align your worldview with God's reality.

To pursue your destiny, you need only to pursue your identity. If you know *who* God created, you'll also know *why* He created you. To know *who* is to know *why* because knowing your identity means you know your uniqueness. If you know how you're unique and gifted, you'll know how God expects you to contribute—you'll know your destiny.

To have an accurate worldview, you must ask God to let you see with His eyes, and ask the Holy Spirit to illuminate the truth of the Bible. What does the Bible say about who God is and who you are?

To have healthy desires, you must set your priorities to match God's. Desire what God created you to desire.

To respond well to God's reality, you must allow the crises in your life to shape you into your God-given identity.

To be content with your identity, you must believe God is all-good and created you as a worthwhile person.

You must accept your identity without reservation.

You must accept the reality God has given you.

Listen and hear.

God is calling your name.

God is calling you *To Identity and Beyond!*

Chapter 16 — Stage 5: Calling Focused

Study Questions

1. What is most important in life? What are you willing to die for?
2. How well do your priorities match your values?
3. How well are you playing the long game, and what can you do to improve?
4. What does advancing God's kingdom mean to you? How strongly do you desire this?
5. What does having an abundant life mean to you? How satisfied are you with your life?
6. If the Kingdom of God is within your midst (Luke 17:21), how can you experience it today?
7. What does it mean to be one with God, one with other believers, and one with your spouse? How are these the same or different?
8. How far can you advance the Kingdom of God without partnering with other believers? How far with partnering?
9. What would it look like for you to partner with other believers?

Chapter 17

Going Beyond

You've come this far, which means you've persevered on this journey to learn how important it is to discover your true identity. Is God tugging on your heart to go beyond?

> *"Go therefore and make disciples of all nations, baptizing them in the name of the Father and of the Son and of the Holy Spirit, teaching them to observe all that I have commanded you."*
> *—Matthew 28:19–20a*

Commit to Living Your Authentic Identity

Are you committed to living your authentic identity? Would you like to join me on the quest of a lifetime—to live the way God intended you to live?

Invest in God's Kingdom

Moving forward with God's Great Commission requires a long-term plan. Instead of thinking of yourself as one piece of rope that must accomplish everything in your lifetime, realize that you're one link in a web of strong chains. Or, put another way, you're one branch connected to the Vine. You matter, but you're not alone.

If every Christian were to disciple ten people in his lifetime and lead them into maturity, and if those ten people also discipled ten others, and so forth, imagine how quickly the church would grow.

As all Christians grow in their identity, the time will pass quickly as God's plans come to fruition. Then we'll all be together in heaven, fully knowing each other and fully knowing God.

Consider what is your specific part in moving God's kingdom forward. Focus on that.

Invest in Your Care and Growth

Commit to discovering and using your identity for God's purposes and glory. As a Christian, you can fulfill the destiny God has planned for you by committing to these four goals:
1. Know yourself better.
2. Know God better.
3. Participate in a Christian community as you help each other pursue knowledge of God and self.
4. Help those outside the church know who they are and who God is.

You'll only be genuinely fulfilled as you discover and act on exactly who God made you to be. To know yourself better, learn your spiritual identity as well as your unique personality.

Join together with other Christians to grasp the full significance of your identity. Help other Christians know themselves and God and allow them to help you know yourself and God.

Here are two questions to ask as you begin your journey, find a direction, and stay on course each day:
1. How are you suppressing or ignoring your authentic self?
2. In what way can you grow toward your authentic self?

Your authentic self is your God-given identity. Your identity is God's greatest gift to you, so go ahead, open it up and discover who you are.

What Next?

What you believe is what you'll act upon. What do you believe about identity? What unanswered questions do you have about identity? You can contact me at mpavlik@nrcounseling.com.

If you have decided to seriously pursue your identity, let me know so I can celebrate with you.

I wrote *Confident Identity* for those who want to work out the details of who they are, showing them how to rebel against who they aren't. *Confident Identity* is a workbook filled with experiential exercises. You can learn more about it in the following section and in the final pages of this book.

Chapter 17 — Going Beyond

Further Study Resources and Help

ToIdentityAndBeyond.com

Visit for: More about identity, including bonus materials. Are you interested in joining a community of other like-minded people to learn your identity? Learn about starting a *To Identity and Beyond* group.

ConfidentIdentity.com

Visit for: More about identity, including bonus materials. I'm planning to have an online assessment based on the ideas explored within this book.

ChristianConcepts.com

Visit for: News and information about upcoming publications and products. Additional material about individual and marital growth. Opportunities to ask questions and post comments.

NewReflectionsCounseling.com

Visit for: Details about specific services like Christian talk-therapy, career counseling, life coaching, and intensive counseling.

MarriageFromRootsToFruits.com

Visit for: Information about my first book on preparing for and having a better marriage.

MattPavlik.pro

Visit for: Learning what else I'm up to as an author, counselor, and software developer.

Feedback

I hope you found *To Identity and Beyond* to be a helpful tool on your growth journey. If you've enjoyed this book, will you consider sharing the message with others?

The study questions included throughout this book make it ideal for a small group or book club. You'll have an opportunity to grow deeper in relationship as you share insights and life struggles with each other.

Reader reviews on Amazon or Goodreads are sincerely appreciated. My Twitter handle is @newreflectionz if you wish to reach out on social media. I also have a Pinterest board:

https://www.pinterest.com/NewReflectionz/confident-identity

I'll gladly receive your comments and feedback about this book. If you have a specific question you're wondering about or need some further direction, don't hesitate to contact me—I'll do the best I can to help. Contact me at mpavlik@nrcounseling.com or visit one of the websites above for more information.

Supplemental Material

Appendix A   **You 2.0 Prayer**

Appendix B   **Identity Affirmations**

Appendix C   **Identity Scriptures**

Appendix D   **Movie List**

                     Selected Bibliography

                     Index of Scriptures

Appendix A — You 2.0 Prayer

Use this prayer to start your gentle climb to loving God:

"Lord Jesus, I know that I have fallen short of Your perfect standard and I don't deserve eternal life. But I believe You paid the full penalty for my sin when You died and rose from the grave. I surrender control of my life to You. Jesus, come into my life, take control of my life, forgive my sins, and save me. I place my trust in You for my salvation, and I accept Your free gift of eternal life. Now, having accepted Your gift, I'm a new creation that will live with You for all eternity. I further grant permission to Your Holy Spirit to help me grow into my true identity."

If this is your heart's prayer, all the blessings of a confident identity are yours.

Appendix B — Identity Affirmations

1. My identity comes from God. My self-image, how positively or negatively I view myself, can change, but my God-given identity is permanent and unchanging.
2. God loves me unconditionally. He's never going to give up on me.
3. Because God is pleased with who I am, I'm good enough as I am. Pretending to be someone I'm not doesn't help anyone. I can't go wrong if I remain true to who God made me to be.
4. God alone has the authority to determine my worth. I'm valuable because God says I am.
5. All voices are powerless to negate who I am. I don't have to allow others to downgrade my self-image.
6. I'm a work in progress. I'm free to experiment with my life to determine the best path for me. I can grow and become more of who God made me to be.
7. No matter how many mistakes I make, there's always a path forward for me. I never have to live without hope.
8. God has forgiven me and taken away my shame. My past wounds and mistakes are important to understand, but I'm not doomed to repeat them.
9. I prefer to be liked by others, but I'll be okay if they don't.
10. I don't have to do what others want or be who they want. Sometimes the most loving action is refusing to put my life on hold despite another's preferences.
11. God wants me to focus only on what I can control. I can choose for myself and allow others to choose for themselves.
12. Whatever I can possibly lose isn't part of my identity. If I lose it, I can thrive without it.
13. I can survive the changes, crises, and consequences that come into my life. I can endure all things through Christ who strengthens me.

14. God created me with needs and desires. He wants me to find healthy ways to meet my needs. I'm not selfish when I'm allowing others to meet my needs.
15. I'm irreplaceable. I have a unique contribution to make. No one else can perform some tasks in the same way I can.
16. God created me to be a blessing to others. As I know and develop who I am, I can share the blessings of Christ.
17. If it's beyond my purpose, it's not my responsibility. I accept what I can't do as much as I appreciate what I can do.
18. God wants me to pursue His specific purposes for creating me. I have a destiny to fulfill. No one can cancel my destiny.
19. My identity is who I am. My destiny is where I'm going. My circumstances don't determine my identity or my destiny. I already have all I need to experience peace and joy.
20. No weapon formed against me shall prosper. There are many plans, but the Lord's purpose will prevail. I will live forever.

Appendix C — Identity Scriptures

Designs to harm me shall fail.	Isaiah 54:17
I have plans, a hope, and a future.	Jeremiah 29:11
I am free because of the truth.	John 8:32
I have abundant life.	John 10:10
I know Christ, His voice, and He knows me.	John 10:14–16
I am dead to sin but alive to God.	Romans 6:2, 11
I am free from all condemnation.	Romans 8:1
I am a child of God; God is my Father; I am an heir of God, co-heir with Christ.	Romans 8:16–17
I am a conqueror.	Romans 8:37
I have the mind of Christ.	1 Corinthians 2:16
I always triumph in Christ.	2 Corinthians 2:14
I am a new creation.	2 Corinthians 5:17
I am the righteousness of God through Christ.	2 Corinthians 5:21
I have all I need to abound in every good work.	2 Corinthians 9:8
I am redeemed from the curse of the law.	Galatians 3:13–14
I am holy and blameless in God's sight.	Ephesians 1:4
I am redeemed and forgiven.	Ephesians 1:7
I am sealed with the Holy Spirit, a deposit guaranteeing my inheritance.	Ephesians 1:13–14
I am saved by God's grace, not by anything I do.	Ephesians 2:9
I am God's workmanship, created in Christ Jesus to do good works.	Ephesians 2:10
I am the dwelling place of God.	Ephesians 2:19–22
I am being made into God's image—the completion of which is guaranteed.	Philippians 1:6
I can endure everything through God who gives me strength.	Philippians 4:13
My God will meet all my needs according to the glorious riches in Christ Jesus.	Philippians 4:19

TO IDENTITY AND BEYOND

I have been rescued from the dominion of darkness, brought into Christ's kingdom.	Colossians 1:13
I am complete in Christ.	Colossians 2:10
I am free from the written code, the law, and its regulations.	Colossians 2:14
I am chosen and loved by God.	1 Thessalonians 1:4
Fear is not my practice.	2 Timothy 1:7
I am born again of imperishable seed. I will live forever.	1 Peter 1:23
I am a royal priest. I belong to God.	1 Peter 2:4–10
My worries are over.	1 Peter 5:7

Appendix D — Movie List

You can watch these movies to explore your understanding of identity.

For each movie, I've included a few words to describe its theme and any cautions. The ratings span from G to R. The R movies contain depictions of intense violence or trauma. These depictions are generally necessary to tell the story, but some of these movies have offensive material. If you have concerns, research the movies before you watch them.

Use these questions to help you organize your experience into a plan for growth:
1. What are the main themes and principles of the movie?
2. With which character do you identify most? Least?
3. How does the movie speak to the reason you're reading this book?
4. How does the movie challenge your understanding of identity?
5. In what ways did the movie inspire you?
6. How will you live differently based on what you learned?

Movie	Year	Themes	Rating
The Lion King	1994	Finding your identity	G
Toy Story	1995	Discovering and accepting who you really are	G
Curious George	2006	Innocence; attachment	G
Beauty and the Beast (Disney)	1991	Intimacy; beauty isn't skin deep	G
Up	2009	Enjoying the moment you have; no regrets	PG
Inside Out	2015	Emotion's role in healing	PG
The Ultimate Gift	2006	Finding meaning and purpose	PG
Evan Almighty	2007	Leading, following; faith, trust	PG
The Truman Show	1998	Confidence vs. self-doubt	PG
Groundhog Day	1993	Self-awareness; growth is fun	PG
Back to the Future trilogy	1985	Confidence vs self-doubt; self-control	PG

TO IDENTITY AND BEYOND

The Incredibles	2004	Distinct abilities; teamwork	PG
Bridge to Terabithia	2007	True friendship	PG
How to Train Your Dragon	2010	Be yourself; use your strengths	PG
Simon Birch	1998	Purpose; significance	PG
Prince of Egypt	1998	Choosing between earthly and true identity	PG
The Butterfly Circus	2009	Overcoming limitations	NR (PG)
A Beautiful Mind	2001	Sorting fact from fiction	PG-13
Ragamuffin	2014	Inadequacy; addiction	PG-13
The Lord of the Rings trilogy	2001	Perseverance; teamwork, trust	PG-13
I'm Not Ashamed	2016	Making Jesus a priority	PG-13
The Dark Knight (Batman trilogy)	2005	What is identity?	PG-13
The Passion of the Christ	2004	Jesus's life and sacrifice	R; graphic depiction of crucifixion
The Matrix	1999	Choose what is true over what is false	R; sci-fi violence and language
The King's Speech	2010	Confidence vs. self-doubt	R; some language
Gladiator	2000	Self-sacrifice; legacy	R; war violence
Slumdog Millionaire	2008	Growing up without parents; perseverance	R; graphic pictures of abuse, neglect

Additional movies to consider: Sybil, Identity, Dances with Wolves, Nacho Libre.

Selected Bibliography

Allender, Dan B., and Tremper Longman III. *The Cry Of The Soul.* NavPress, 1994.
Anderson, Neil T. *Victory over The Darkness.* Regal Books, 1990.
Benner, David G. *The Gift of Being Yourself.* InterVarsity Press, 2004.
Benner, David. *Surrender To Love.* InterVarsity Press, 2003.
Bevere, Lisa. *Without Rival.* Baker Publishing Group, 2016.
Carter, Les, and Frank Minirth. *The Anger Workbook.* Thomas Nelson Publishers, 1993.
Clarke, Jean Illsley, and Connie Dawson. *Growing Up Again.* Hazelden, 1998.
Clinton, Tim, and Joshua Straub. *God Attachment.* Howard Books, 2010.
Cloud, Henry. *Changes That Heal.* HarperPaperbacks, 1995.
—. *The Law Of Happiness.* Howard Books, 2011.
Cloud, Henry, and John Townsend. *How People Grow.* Zondervan, 2001.
Colson, Charles. *Loving God.* Zondervan, 1987.
Covey, Stephen R. *The 7 Habits Of Highly Effective People.* Simon & Schuster, 1990.
Crabb, Larry. *Inside Out.* Navpress, 1988.
—. *Men & Women.* Zondervan Publishing House, 1991.
Dolan, Yvonne. *One Small Step.* Authors Choice Press, 2000.
Eldredge, John. *Beautiful Outlaw.* Hachette Book Group, 2011.
Ells, Alfred H. *One-way Relationships Workbook.* Thomas Nelson Publishers, 1992.
Erikson, Erik H. *Childhood and Society.* W W Norton & Company, 1993.
—. *Identity Youth and Crisis.* 1968.
Groom, Nancy. *From Bondage to Bonding.* NavPress, 1991.
Hemfelt, Robert, and Paul Warren. *Kids Who Carry Our Pain.* Thomas Nelson, 1990.
Jakes, T. D. *Destiny.* Hachette Book Group, 2015.
—. *Identity.* Destiny Image, 2015.

—. *Instinct.* Hachette Book Group, 2014.
Jung, C. G. *Aspects of the Masculine.* Princeton University Press, 1989.
Lawson, Steven J. *When All Hell Breaks Loose.* NavPress, 1993.
McGee, Robert. *The Search For Significance.* Thomas Nelson, 1998.
Morgan, Richard L. *Remembering Your Story.* 2002.
Pascal, Blaise. *Pascal's Pensees.* 1958.
Pavlik, Matt. *Confident Identity.* Christian Concepts, 2017.
Posthuma, David A. *Made for a Mission.* 2008.
Pulaski, Mary Ann Spencer. *Understanding Piaget.* Harper & Row, 1971.
Rath, Tom. *Strengths Finder 2.0.* 2007.
Seamands, David. *Living With Your Dreams.* Victor, 1990.
Shapiro, Francine. *Getting Past Your Past.* Rodale, 2012.
Siegel, Daniel J. *The Developing Mind.* The Guilford Press, 2012.
Smedes, Lewis. *Shame & Grace.* HarperOne, 1993.
Smith, Hyrum W. *The 10 Natural Laws of Successful Time and Life Management.* Warner Books, 1994.
Springle, Pat. *Trusting.* Servant Publications, 1994.
Thompson, Curt. *Anatomy of The Soul.* Tyndale House Publishers, 2010.
Thrall, Bill, Bruce McNicol, and John Lynch. *TrueFaced.* 2004.
Wardle, Terry. "Formational Prayer Seminar." Healing Care Ministries (healingcare.org), 2009.
—. *Identity Matters.* Leafwood Publishers, 2017.
—. *Wounded.* Leafwood, 2005.
Warren, Rick. *Purpose Driven Life.* 2002.
Wilson, Sandra. *Released From Shame.* InterVarsity Press, 2002.
—. *Shame Free Parenting.* InterVarsity Press, 1992.

Index of Scriptures

Genesis
- 2:25 — 174
- 3:1–5 — 173
- 3:5 — 74
- 18 — 77
- 32 — 77

Exodus
- 32 — 90
- 33:18–23 — 32

Leviticus

Numbers
- 12:3, 7b — 89

Deuteronomy
- 31:6 — 48

Joshua
- 24:14–15 — 92
- 24:16–18 — 92

Judges
- 2 — 92

Ruth

1 Samuel
- 17:38–40 — 175

2 Samuel

1 Kings

2 Kings

1 Chronicles

2 Chronicles

Ezra

Nehemiah

Esther

Job
- 2:9–10 — 52
- 13:15 — 159

Psalm
- 37:4 — 57
- 138:8 — 122
- 139 — 15, 41, 112, 122
- 139:7–10 — 41
- 139:16 — 15, 122

Proverbs
- 16:26 — 40
- 18:24 — 48
- 30:7–9 — 64

Ecclesiastes
- 5:8–20 — 38, 51
- 7:4 — 73

Song of Solomon

Isaiah
- 9:6 — 2
- 14:12–15 — 76
- 41:10 — 49
- 54:17 — 201

Jeremiah
- 29:11 — 122, 201
- 29:13 — 83

Lamentations

Ezekiel

Daniel

Hosea

Joel

Amos

Obadiah

Jonah

Micah

Nahum

Habakkuk

Zephaniah

Haggai

Zechariah

Malachi

Matthew			10:10	7, 57, 201
4:8–10	75		10:14–16	201
5:3, 6	52		10:38–42	45
5:13–16	172		11:21–27	45
6:9–13	6		13:8–9	84
6:21	58		14:6, 16	25
6:24	144		14:12	171
6:32	54		14:16–17	7
6:33	7		14:18–20	25
7:7	16, 46		15:5	144
7:7–11	46		15:12–13	94
11:28–30	81		15:14–17	80
13:44	83		16:13	7
15:21–28	83		16:33	37
16:17	31		17:3	2
19:20–22	66		18:17	80
25:14–30	93		21:15–17	81
25:23	94		21:20–22	176
26:41	168	Acts		
27:3–5	68	9:1–7		76
28:19–20a	6, 191	17:26		27
Mark		Romans		
4:15	2	5:3		37
14:32–38	95	6:2, 11		201
Luke		6:9–11		169
10:27	90	6:13		161
15	138, 145, 146	6:23		2
		8		97
15:13–16	145	8:1		59, 160, 201
15:28–30	146	8:16–17		201
17:21	189	8:17		160
19:5–6	85	8:18		59
19:9–10	85	8:22		32
22:3–4	68	8:29		17, 122
John		8:37		201
3:16	97	14:17		6
4:13–14	56	1 Corinthians		
4:24	49	2:6–16		27
4:31–38	51	2:16		201
5:19	169	7:29–31		58
6:35	82	9:22b–27		92
8:1–11	123	13:12		32
8:32	201			
8:44	2			

TO IDENTITY AND BEYOND

208

Index of Scriptures

2 Corinthians
- 2:14 — 201
- 4:16–17 — 124
- 5:17 — 201
- 5:21 — 201
- 9:8 — 201
- 12:2 — 91
- 13:14 — xii

Galatians
- 1:10 — 175
- 2:20 — 25
- 3:13–14 — 201

Ephesians
- 1:4 — 201
- 1:7 — 201
- 1:13–14 — 201
- 2:8–9 — 2, 97
- 2:9 — 201
- 2:10 — 5, 48, 122, 201
- 2:19–22 — 201
- 4:14 — 33
- 4:22–24 — 173
- 6:12 — 62

Philippians
- 1:6 — 19, 91, 201
- 1:21 — 58
- 3:13–14 — 92
- 4:11–13 — 56
- 4:13 — 201
- 4:19 — 7, 201

Colossians
- 1:13 — 202
- 2:10 — 202
- 2:14 — 202

1 Thessalonians
- 1:4 — 202

2 Thessalonians

1 Timothy
- 6:6–11 — 50

2 Timothy
- 1:7 — 202

Titus

Philemon

Hebrews
- 1:2–3 — 27
- 2:17 — 94
- 4:14–16 — 97
- 4:16 — 84
- 7:24–25 — 97
- 7:25 — 84
- 10:10, 14 — xiii, 78
- 10:39 — 97
- 11:13–16 — 182
- 11:24–26 — 94
- 12 — 57, 60
- 12:3 — 97
- 13:5–6 — 52

James
- 1:1–4 — 90
- 1:2–4 — 37
- 2:17 — 79, 169
- 2:23 — 88
- 4:4–6 — 71

1 Peter
- 1:23 — 202
- 2:2–3 — 82
- 2:4–10 — 202
- 3:15 — 33
- 5:7 — 202
- 5:8 — 62
- 5:10 — 80, 122

2 Peter

1 John
- 4:18 — 92
- 4:19 — 90
- 5:10–21 — 97

2 John

3 John

Jude

Revelation

About Matt Pavlik

Matt Pavlik is a licensed professional clinical counselor who wants each individual restored to their true identity. In addition to *To Identity and Beyond* (see ToIdentityAndBeyond.com), he has authored two workbooks: one on identity and the other on marriage (see ConfidentIdentity.com and MarriageFromRootsToFruits.com). He has more than 15 years of experience counseling individuals and couples at his Christian private practice, New Reflections Counseling, (see NewReflectionsCounseling.com). He completed his Masters in Clinical Pastoral Counseling from Ashland Theological Seminary and his Bachelors in Computer Science from the University of Illinois. Matt and his wife Georgette have been married since 1999 and live with their four children in Centerville, Ohio.

Matt's mission is to use the wisdom he receives from God to help others understand God's design for life. Learn more at ChristianConcepts.com.

Also by Matt Pavlik

Confident Identity

Jessica Buczek, MS, LPCC had this to say:

Have you ever read a book that leaves you in a thoughtful place of contemplation long after the last page has been turned and the book is closed? *Confident Identity* is that kind of book. It's a conversation-starter, a thought-generator, and a game-changer.

Days after reading its final pages, I found myself deliberately and intentionally processing the content of this book. Thinking through my personality, pondering my gifts, and praying through my God-given and life-shaped identity, I couldn't shake the significance of its words. I felt a sense of purpose after reading its words—a driving challenge to explore, expand, and exercise my identity for not only myself but also for the edification of those around me and for the glorification of my Heavenly Father.

This resource does a wonderful job of providing the reader with mini therapeutic sessions that can be done in the confines of a home, over a cup of coffee with a trusted friend, in a church community group, or even in the safety of a therapist's office. As a therapist myself, this will be in a quick-to-reach spot in my office, as I see this book being a helpful clinical resource when thinking through treatment plans and case conceptualization for those who are struggling in understanding, defining, and forming their identity.

Marriage From Roots to Fruits

Will W Alejandro, MDiv, MA had this to say:

As I read through Matt's book, *Marriage From Roots to Fruits*, I felt hopeful. I thought of all the couples I have met along the way who looked at their relationship, present and future, with a sense of futility and hopelessness. The author gives details of God's design for a healthy relationship, with very practical tools, filled with real life examples to encourage them along the path of healing and living victoriously.

I have not read a book (manual) like it before. I believe it will help couples who are at the point of hopelessness and emotional pain to truly heal. I also feel it is very applicable for married couples who feel good about the relationship they have but want to have a stronger and deeper relationship with God and with themselves. Matt designed the book to be a tool for pastors and counselors, to use as a guide for premarital counseling, and to help hurting marriages. I feel that this book is a must-read for all caregivers.

www.ingramcontent.com/pod-product-compliance
Lightning Source LLC
Chambersburg PA
CBHW050632300426
44112CB00012B/1763